Mirror, mirror on the wall,
I'm a maiden after all!

RAISING

MAIDENS

OF VIRTUE

A STUDY OF FEMININE LOVELINESS
FOR MOTHERS AND DAUGHTERS

by

STACY MCDONALD

www.booksonthepath.com

Raising Maidens of Virtue: A Study of Feminine Loveliness for Mothers and Daughters
Copyright © 2004 by James and Stacy McDonald

Published in the United States by
Books on the Path
P.O. Box 436
Barker, TX 77413
www.booksonthepath.com
281-492-6050

Library of Congress Cataloging-in-Publication Data
McDonald, Stacy D.
Library of Congress Control Number: 2004096987
ISBN 0-9743390-1-6

Color Illustrations by Johannah Bluedorn
Page Design and Typesetting by James McDonald, VI
Cover Design by Tobias' Outerwear for Books
Cover image and fine art illustrations supplied by the Art Renewal Center, www.artrenewal.org.
Scripture are taken from The Holy Bible: King James Version. 1995. Logos Bible Software: Bellingham, WA. www.logos.com/demo Used
by Permission.

This study is dedicated to you, my own precious fair maidens: Christa, Tiffany, Melissa, Jessica, Abigail, Virginia Grace, and Emma Katherine. May the Lord grant you wisdom and grace as you pass through the merry gates of childhood into the breathtaking garden of godly womanhood. Remember that your faithfulness to your family now as sisters and daughters is a clear reflection of the devotion you will have in serving your future families as wives and mothers. I love you, I thank God for you, and I pray fervently that you will walk faithfully before God and man as true Maidens of Virtue.

Raising Maidens of Virtue is also dedicated to the Christian maidens across the globe who are responding to God's call to purity and feminine loveliness. Though there may be moments when you feel like a stranger in a strange land, though you may walk alone at times in godly wholesomeness, be encouraged—you are doing a good work. You are worshipping our Lord through your godly deportment; you are obeying His Word by your steadfast purity; and you are honoring your parents by your winsome femininity. May God be glorified through you in this generation, and by your faithfulness may He grant hope to the generations to come.

IN HIS SERVICE,

STACY MCDONALD

CONTENTS

FOREWORD

*J*ust what *is* a maiden? When we hear the word, do we picture a medieval princess strumming a lute in some fantastical castle? Or perhaps we imagine a prim and proper nineteenth-century schoolmarm with every hair in place. Maybe we're even cynical enough to scoff at the very notion of maidenhood and decide that it is a quaint and outdated concept we are well rid of. After all, doesn't being a maiden imply that a girl will live a secluded life, shuttered away from the world and contemplating her virtues alone?

God's Word gives us many beautiful word pictures of young women. Perhaps the best known (and often least discussed!) in Christian families is the picture of the woman in the Song of Solomon. The writer describes his wife as a walled garden full of delicious fruits, beautiful flowers, rich perfumes, and sweet springs of water (4:12-16). The wall protects her from intruders and preserves her beauties for her husband—but the wall is not ugly or "restrictive." Indeed, the garden could not remain untrammeled and unharmed without the wall. She has been lovingly guarded since maidenhood, tenderly cared for and prepared for the one gardener (whether her spouse upon marriage or the Lord if she is called to remain single).

At the end of the Song of Solomon, the Shulamite men ask what they should do for their young sister. The answer is to cover her walls with silver and build up her door with boards of cedar. Here we can see that it is the job of brothers not only to protect the purity of their sisters but also to make the "wall" of protection beautiful at the same time. Maidenly modesty is not dour and unsmiling. It is not shadowy or fearful. It does not suppress God-given femininity. Rather, modesty and propriety shine like silver and sparkle like pure spring water from a fountain. But these virtues cannot survive alone. They require champions and bold protectors—fathers and brothers who will guard maidenhood even as godly mothers and sisters cultivate it and nourish it.

But where have all the bold knights gone? Where are the pure maidens who inspire them to heroism?

It is easy to look at the culture around us and point fingers as we ponder the lost virtues of maidenhood. Even tiny girls walk around in "hooker chic" with jaded looks in their eyes, their innocence trampled upon by the media, pop culture, and peer pressure. "Where are their fathers?" we might ask. "What is her mother *thinking* to dress her that way?"

But we need look no further than our own hearts to see the root of the problem. The sin that despises maidenhood is within all of us. From the moment Satan tempted Eve to sell her God-given innocence for a dime-store version of "wisdom," we have been looking in all the wrong places for love, acceptance, and beauty. This folly has manifested itself in varying ways throughout the ages; that it is now so overwhelmingly obvious is due largely, I believe, to our media-saturated world. Where women once "made over" old outfits to wear again, we now witness trends changing by the week as Miss Celebrity Idol struts her stuff across the magazine covers at the local checkout. And it isn't just the clothing styles that morph with bewildering speed. The very values we have cherished as a Christian nation—protecting the innocent, guarding purity, training boys to be godly gentlemen— have been tossed aside like yesterday's blue jeans.

How can we cherish maidenhood in a world seemingly gone mad? How can we imitate the beauties of Scriptural models without becoming pietists who are proud of our own feeble works? Is it truly possible to cultivate maidenhood without seeming "holier than thou" when even the Church seems reluctant to speak about purity and modesty today? What about girls who do not live in an ideal environment and who struggle alone against peer pressure and cultural images that war against godly propriety?

Stacy McDonald has given us a wonderful tool to reclaim maidenly virtues *as families.* Written primarily to mothers and daughters, this book is, nevertheless, important reading for fathers who desire to guard their daughters and encourage their God-given femininity in a godly way. And for young women who have no godly guardians, this book comes alongside as a friend to point the way and provide encouragement. Mrs. McDonald focuses on maidenhood from several different perspectives, calling our attention to heart matters like guarding the tongue and extending hospitality, but also showing the importance of grooming and dress in the context of loving our neighbor and honoring the Lord with our bodies. The study questions and suggested activities help foster a love for tangible beauty and strengthen our desire to protect the blessing of maidenly innocence even while we live in the world and witness to it.

Our world desperately needs to see the beautiful antithesis that is the gospel. Christians need to declare to the lost that femininity is a wonderful part of the image of God: "So God created man in his own image, in the image of God created he him; male and female created he them" (Genesis 1:27). As our culture drifts into greater androgyny, what an opportunity we have to show the God-designed delights of womanliness! We need young women who cherish their purity and desire to honor their parents through chaste behavior, speech, and dress. We need girls of *character* who cultivate their minds and emotions to reflect God's design with joy, intelligence, and delight.

What a privilege to be maidens in the service of the Lord! God loves the beauty He has created, and every young woman can be a princess in His house: "Hearken, O daughter, and consider, and incline thine ear; forget also thine own people, and thy father's house; so shall the king greatly desire thy beauty: for he is thy Lord; and worship thou him…The king's daughter is all glorious within: her clothing is of wrought gold. She shall be brought unto the king in raiment of needlework: the virgins her companions that follow her shall be brought unto thee. With gladness and rejoicing shall they be brought: they shall enter into the king's palace" (Psalm 45:10-11, 13-15).

May we give our daughters a vision of maidenhood that is every bit as glorious and joyful as this one! May we help them to treasure their femininity and cultivate the godly beauty of a quiet spirit as we prepare them for womanhood.

MRS. JENNIE CHANCEY

AT HOME

ACKNOWLEDGMENTS

*A*s I look back over the tapestry of my life, it is easy to see how God used the foolish sins and painful experiences of my past to mold, shape, and prepare me for this study. Along with that, the sobering realization that I was responsible to successfully raise pure and godly daughters in a morally polluted culture caused a longing in my heart for something better—something clean, fresh, and lovely. The result was a vision for our daughters, a vision for a sacred return to feminine maidenhood and purity.

Thank you to my beloved husband, James, who is truly my knight in shining armor, my protector, my friend, and my greatest encourager.

Without the daily lessons I am learning with my own seven maiden daughters—Christa, Tiffany, Melissa, Jessica, Abigail, Virginia Grace, and Emma Katherine—I would have nothing to write. To them I am grateful, especially since they not only shared my vision by living it out, but they labored along with me physically by pitching in with the extra workload at home while I wrote this study. They even helped me write or edit many of the chapters.

My thankfulness also extends to my two sons, James Michael VI and Caleb Beauchamp, who are rising up as valiant knights in their own right— my oldest, who has worked hard scanning the images and providing all the layout and design work for this book, and my youngest, who is still drawing beautiful castles that he promises to build for me one day when I am "old." May you both be blessed with wives who are true maidens of virtue and worth.

I thank God for my friends, Mary Jo Tate, Mary Alice Churchman, Jennie Chancey, Marti Pieper, Laurie Bluedorn, and Nan Keen for their invaluable assistance in editing, counseling, and advising. Thank you for your time and for sharing this vision with me.

Most of all I thank our Heavenly Father. Though I wasted my own maiden years, God in His mercy chose to redeem me in His timing and restore what the locusts had eaten. He has given me a future and a hope and granted that our own maiden daughters may shine like a light on a hill— penetrating the darkness around them to reach a lost and dying world. For this answered prayer, I am most humbly and profoundly grateful.

Ye are the light of the world. A city that is set on an hill cannot be hid. Neither do men light a candle, and put it under a bushel, but on a candlestick; and it giveth light unto all that are in the house. Let your light so shine before men, that they may see your good works, and glorify your Father which is in heaven (Matthew 5:14-16).

INTRODUCTION

*That our daughters may be as corner stones, polished after the similitude of a palace
(Psalm 144:12).*

A MESSAGE TO MOTHER

Remember those precious days of cuddling your helpless nursing babe—
the chubby-fisted infant who needed you so? Now that same dimpled
hand has gracefully transformed into the slender one of a competent
young woman and no longer grasps her mother's—at least not as tightly as she did during her lullaby years.

Once upon a time, this little one needed the nourishment and comfort of milk, the
kind offered by an adoring mother. Now, to become the mature woman God desires, she
requires a different kind of milk: the Milk of the Word, pure and good.

As we grow, we find that God always has more for us to learn. He designed a mother's body to produce nourishment for her infant in a convenient, easily digestible form.
Likewise, God in His infinite wisdom gave us a living Word to nourish and strengthen each
of us in every new stage of life (1 Corinthians 3:2).

Although your daughter has always needed God's Word, her training in a specific
area of God's truth (Titus 2:4-5) has now become imperative. This beautiful creature,
this lovely young girl who radiates the very essence of purity and hope, now depends upon
you to help illuminate her path to godly womanhood. Humbling? Challenging? Most
assuredly.

As our young maidens journey through life, they will meet many different people
and hear a myriad of strange doctrines and teachings. Our daughters must know what
they believe and why they believe it, or they will find themselves "tossed to and fro"
with every new philosophy that comes along (Ephesians 4:14). They must learn to

search the Scriptures, under the protection and guidance of their God-given authorities, and discover for themselves the beautiful picture of womanhood presented in God's Word.

Through stories, allegories, conversational teachings, and illustrations, *Raising Maidens of Virtue* covers topics such as guarding the tongue, jealousy, idleness, sibling relationships, honoring parents, contentment, modesty, femininity, purity, cleanliness, deportment, trust, and biblical beauty.

Much more than a fill-in-the-blank Bible study, *Raising Maidens of Virtue* is a tool for mothers to use in training their young maidens to think biblically. Older and younger women who partner to study this book together will deepen their relationships and make lasting memories while reasoning together and discussing the vital areas that encompass godly womanhood.

Who Should Read This Book?

This book is designed primarily to be used by mothers and daughters or by mature, godly women and the growing young ladies they are mentoring. However, I have included a few additional creative ways in which this book can be used.

> ✤ **Mothers and Daughters** - Plan a special time with your daughter(s) to read and enjoy mother-daughter time together. I recommend beginning this study with young ladies who realize that one day soon, they will be women. Only you know when your maiden is ready, but daughters between the ages of 12 and 18, along with their mothers, will most likely gain the most from this study.
>
> This will be a time of growth and intimacy that each of you will remember forever. Make it a time of celebration and relationship-building. Set a cozy, quiet spot in the corner with some herbal tea and cookies. See if Dad can watch the boys for an hour while you share this special feminine-focused time together.
>
> ✤ **Virtuous Maiden Tea** - Host a regular Tea Time in your home and invite other women and their daughters to join you. Become a Titus 2 teacher and share what God has taught you, using your Bible and this book as tools. It

might be fun to decorate with lacy napkins, china, decorative tea sets, flowers, music boxes, or other items of beauty and femininity. Make it special!

ᔐ **Titus 2 on Wheels** - If your own children are older, consider becoming a Titus 2 mentor. Offer to visit a mother who has daughters, but who has never been taught about godly womanhood herself. Surely she would appreciate someone willing to assist her in training her own daughters in the area of biblical femininity and virtue.

Help such a mother pass on a godly legacy of maidenhood to her daughters. If she has younger children at home, she might really appreciate a regular (or flexible) meeting in her own home. Ask her where she would like to meet and plan it. However, be careful not to undermine the mother's authority in any way.

Remember that God has orchestrated each family by His will and for His own purpose. You are never to usurp the authority of a young maiden's parents or disregard the wishes of her father. It is only your duty to share the truths of Scripture and aid the mother in her task of mothering.

ᔐ **Virtuous Maiden Partners** – I highly encourage readers to use this book with a godly older woman, preferably a mother or grandmother, as a mentor. However, studying the book with a partnership of maidens can also prove very helpful. Certainly, seek out a godly female role model who will challenge and encourage you. Nevertheless, if you lack a mentor who will do the study *with* you, don't despair. Trust God to direct your learning and pray that He will protect you from error.

ᔐ **Lone Maidens** – It is always easier to learn when you have a teacher; however, it is possible to benefit from this study on your own. God has given us families and brothers and sisters in the Lord to teach, exhort, protect, encourage, love, and correct us, so it makes sense that studying together is preferred to studying alone. When we work apart from the guidance of those wiser than ourselves, we risk falling into error and we cannot function as a complete and healthy body.

Yet there will be those who find themselves in unique and temporary situations. For instance, a daughter who has lost her mother to death, divorce, or sin may also be temporarily set apart from a church family or godly female influences. I encourage her to remember God's promises of care and mercy for those in such situations:

When my father and my mother forsake me, then the LORD will take me up.
(Psalm 27:10)

Can a woman forget her sucking child, that she should not have compassion on the son of her womb? yea, they may forget, yet will I not forget thee.
(Isaiah 49:15)

A father of the fatherless, and a judge of the widows, is God in his holy habitation. God setteth the solitary in families: he bringeth out those which are bound with chains: but the rebellious dwell in a dry land. (Psalm 68:5-6)

Ask God to bring you a mentor who will direct you in the paths of righteousness. He knows your situation and is already faithfully watching over you.

ॐ **Sunday School** – Again, it is preferable to have mothers involved, so daughters and mothers should be encouraged to join the class together if this study is to be used in a Sunday School or other group setting. Teaching daughters separately from their own mothers may only serve to further fragment the family and usurp the parents' authority in the home. The goal should be to train and encourage mothers to teach their *own* daughters, remembering that many mothers may need to be taught as well.

Ꞙow Jo Use Jhis Book

Although this is a biblical study, it is not meant to be a workbook. It is designed to be read aloud with ample time to discuss and contemplate what you are learning. Take turns reading and enjoy your time together. Make it a special occasion set apart from your other activities. You will find suggestions for a Literary Luncheon, a Historical Women Tea, and a precious memory-making scrapbook, as well as other relationship-building projects and activities.

While it is not mandatory, I highly recommend making a scrapbook to accompany your study. As you will discover when reading the instructions in the project section in the back, it does not have to be extravagant or expensive. You may choose to simply fill and decorate an inexpensive binder with heavy stock paper, or you may prefer a more elaborate method, but I think you will find that organizing your thoughts and memories in a scrapbook or notebook of some kind will enrich your study more than you ever dreamed possible.

The more creative you become with your study, the more memorable it will be. Your time together should be a time of sweet fellowship and growth—a time to explore the truth of feminine beauty and purity while enjoying crafts and creativity.

Don't be surprised if you find some parts of this book convicting, unpleasant, or difficult at first. Please do not allow yourself to be offended by things you may not have ever considered. The emotional response of feeling offended may be a sign that this is an area we need to work on. We should make certain that we do not bow up and resist the Holy Spirit's conviction. Pray and ask God to show you through His Word what is true. He is faithful.

Although learning crucial biblical truths may be uncomfortable at times, your study as a whole should be a time of joy and memory making.

How sweet are thy words unto my taste! yea, sweeter than honey to my mouth! Through thy precepts I get understanding: therefore I hate every false way. (Psalm 119:103-104)

Be sure to present what you are learning to the father of the home and ask for his insight. Remember that God has placed him in the position of authority in the family, and he will probably have a lot of wisdom to share.

Beginning with Chapter One, the text will always be addressed to the young maiden unless otherwise indicated by the salutation of "Mother." I use "Mother" to address all mentors, whether or not they are the actual mother of the maiden.

So pour a few cups of herbal tea, light a scented candle, close the parlor door, turn off the ringer on the telephone, and turn on some soft music. Then curl up together in a cozy spot to enjoy this precious time together!

Dear Lord, keep my face turned toward You always. Do not let me covet the habits and fashions of the world, but give me the strength to turn my back on that which would distract me from Your beauty and goodness. Lead me in the way that I should go and do not let me turn away from your path, nor wink at compromise. Amen.

Chapter 1

THE FENCE DWELLERS

Let not thine heart envy sinners: but be thou in the fear of the LORD all the day long. For surely there is an end; and thine expectation shall not be cut off.
(Proverbs 23:17-18)

O nce upon a time, a kind and wise Gardener created a beautiful garden—a sanctuary of splendor with lush, deep green foliage and rich, colorful flowers of every shape, scent, and size. A lovely trellis spanned a cobblestone path, filled with dreamy-scented roses of the softest texture and deepest hues.

Along the quaint path were fragrant herbs, carefully chosen and planted so they would work and grow well together, all with different textures and shapes. Some had long, soft, feathery leaves; others were full and spiky; a few were bushy and short. Nonetheless, each one had its own unique beauty and purpose in his garden, and the sight and scent of the choreographed blend made it a treasure to visit and brought great joy and satisfaction to the Gardener.

Next to the beautiful garden was a rock quarry, gray and cold. The flowers by the fence nearest the quarry began to turn their faces down toward the rocks on the other side and wonder what it would be like to be strong and smooth.

It was true that rocks had no roots, but the flowers did not really care about roots. Who could see those? It would be much nicer to be big and strong so everyone could behold their powerful shape.

As they gazed upon the gray lifeless rocks, the flowers began to covet the rocks' strength and coolness. They grew discontent with their purpose and design and began to despise the beautiful colors and delicate leaves and petals with which they were adorned. No longer were they satisfied with their own simple beauty. The wayward flowers rejected their delicate leaves and vibrant colors and instead wished to be made of stone—desiring only the strength, weight, and power of the granite. These errant flowers became known as the Fence Dwellers.

The Fence Dwellers began to rip off their beautiful petals and leaves and refused to produce seed. After all, the rocks did not produce seed, so why should they sacrifice in such a selfless manner? The Fence Dwellers covered themselves in clay in order to hide their vibrant colors. Soon they began to crouch low to the ground, trying desperately to resemble the rocks they so deeply admired.

As the older herbs, ivies, and bushes that lived farther inside the garden began to notice the strange behavior of the flowers, they laughed. How foolish the flowers looked: barren of petals, covered in clay, attempting to be something they were not.

But soon, the new seedlings within the garden began to listen to the stories of the Fence Dwellers. And as they grew, they too tore their own delicate petals and dusted themselves with clay—halfway up their stems; they were not yet as daring as the Fence Dwellers who were tempted daily with the sight of the rocks.

The young plants desperately wished they could uproot and live next to the quarry like the Fence Dwellers so they too could see the magnificent boulders and witness the impressive strength of stone.

Something about the boldness of the Fence Dwellers and the stories they told the younger plants of the garden caused a strange spirit of yearning throughout the yard . . . and things began to change.

Within a short period of time, the vibrant color and stunning beauty of the garden were covered in mire. Instead of the sweet perfume of lavender, rosemary, lemon verbena, and blooming flowers, the stench of decay prevailed. The birds looked elsewhere for a home. They were not interested in sheltering their young in a place void of greenery and lacking in beauty. The bees, butterflies, and other insects and wildlife found little nourishment here any more and visited the garden less and less often.

Surprisingly, the Fence Dwellers did not realize they were shriveled and dying. Their bald heads were stripped of petals, and the clay was suffocating their stems—yet they still yearned to be something they were never intended to be. They were blinded by their own vain desires and remained with their faces toward the quarry—turned forever from the Gardener (Proverbs 28:14).

The Gardener walked sadly through his creation and sighed. He noticed the tender plants with clay halfway up their stems and missing petals—the result of a self-imposed deed. He shook his head in dismay.

"Why have you covered yourselves in clay and removed your petals?" cried the Gardener. "I have created you in the way of my choosing—for my own purpose. But you have rejected my ways and set your eyes upon foreigners and have adorned yourself in mud and grime. You have ravaged and exposed your own bodies.

"Do you not know that you belong to me? This was a wicked and foolish deed. You have emulated the Fence Dwellers and have followed after those preferring death. They have chosen cold and hard barrenness over the true beauty of a warm and tender life-giving existence. Do not attempt to mimic those of the quarry or their followers—those who never belonged to me. There you will find only death and desolation."

The plants of the garden shivered and hid their faces; however, the Fence Dwellers did not hear the words of the Gardener, for they were no more. The plants who belonged to the Gardener solemnly watched as the last remnant of the Fence Dwellers' decomposing stems blew quietly over the fence to rest upon a large boulder. Here the scorching sun would finish the job of destruction until nothing remained.

Fret not thyself because of evil men, neither be thou envious at the wicked; For there shall be no reward to the evil man; the candle of the wicked shall be put out. (Proverbs 24:19-20)

Joy in the Morning

The Gardener turned to his creation tenderly. Silently a raindrop landed on the fragile leaf of a basil plant. Three more brushed the buds of a rosebush. Soon a torrent of raindrops poured from the sky, cleansing and refreshing the filthy clay-covered plants. The dandelions wept with joy as the lovers of self repented and turned to the Gardener forevermore. Fresh blossoms opened and the scent of life and beauty filled the air.

The Gardener held out his arms, threw back his head, and laughed a deep, hearty laugh. He was overjoyed with the display of color and renewed health that he had granted his creation. After the rain subsided, the Gardener rested in the shade and summoned the birds to come sing in the branches of a nearby pear tree. Soon more birds followed to nest in the profusion of greenery and scented blossoms. Bursting with life, the young flowers called to the bees to come share their nectar, and the butterflies joined them.

From that day forward, the plants rejoiced in who they were and did not desire to be anything other than what they were called to be. Their only desire and purpose was to please the Gardener and cause him joy forever.

Share Your Heart

- ✎ Who were the Fence Dwellers? What did they have in common with many young people of the world today?
- ✎ Why were the Fence Dwellers uninterested in whether or not they had roots? How is this similar to someone who is unconcerned over the state of her own soul?
- ✎ Discuss why the Fence Dwellers may not have been interested in producing seed (Exodus 1:7, Psalm 128:3-4).

❧ How did the discontentment of the Fence Dwellers affect the younger plants and flowers of the garden?

❧ Have you ever been affected in a similar manner by those who were not seeking God?

❧ Why do you think the younger plants only "tore" their petals slightly and covered themselves in clay "halfway" while the Fence Dwellers "ripped off" their petals and leaves, and completely "covered" themselves in clay?

❧ Mothers, do you see any areas where your young maiden dabbles in forbidden activities "halfway" (music, clothes, rules, moral choices)? If so, discuss the possible effects of this behavior by considering the overall appearance and condition of the garden.

❧ How does this story remind you of the way modern Christians sometimes try to emulate the world? Do you see yourself in this story at all? Discuss with your mother ways you can keep your face turned to the "Gardener" instead of the "quarry."

❧ Read Romans 12:1-2. Discuss what "reasonable service" means and what it means to present ourselves as a living sacrifice to God.

❧ Read and discuss the following Scriptures:
  • Psalm 37:1-6
  • Matthew 6:24
  • 1 John 2:15-17
  • Romans 1:21
  • Romans 8:5-8
  • 1 Peter 1:14
  • Ephesians 5:7-11
  • Revelation 18:4-5

Dear Lord, let my life be a reflection of Your mercy and goodness. Allow a lovely and gentle spirit to shine forth from me. Make my countenance properly express your holiness. Keep me from attempting to glorify myself and help me to instead glorify You in all that I do, wear, and proclaim. Take my life, Lord—do with it what You will, and make me content and joyful always and in everything. Amen.

Chapter 2

MODERN-DAY MAIDENS

I beseech you therefore, brethren, by the mercies of God, that ye present your bodies a liv-ing sacrifice, holy, acceptable unto God, which is your reasonable service. And be not con-formed to this world: but be ye transformed by the renewing of your mind, that ye may prove what is that good, and acceptable, and perfect, will of God. (Romans 12:1-2)

Antique books are much like old friends. Neither one may be as new or strong as they once were, but as the years pass their pages soft-en, their character develops, and their uniqueness is made evident to a new generation. Mysteriously, they grow more precious and even more beau-tiful with age.

One day I was browsing the shelves of an antique bookstore and found a real jewel—a forgotten leather-bound treasure. After blowing the dust off its cover, I observed a tender scene of children playing in a pasture. Like a solitary white rose positioned carefully on the deep velvet lining of a bejeweled box, the charm of the simple painting was curiously enhanced by its gilded, ornate border.

The delightful painting included a young maiden seated upon a blanket, sewing. Her strawberry curls were tied gently behind her back, and her delicately embroidered gown cascaded about her. The look of serenity in her face made me yearn to sit beside her, to share her gentle company, to experience her peaceful afternoon.

Was this innocent vignette of beauty and tranquility a poignant memory belonging only to yesteryear? After all, where were the young lady's skin-tight jeans? And why wasn't her belly button showing? Didn't those frolicking little children in the pasture know they could have been playing video games instead? Do gentle maidens exist today, or did they live only in the vivid imaginations of old-fashioned authors?

Damsels in Distress

One thing you'll notice while reading old books is that young, unmarried women are referred to as virgins, daughters, maidens, and even damsels. At one time a virgin merely meant a woman who had never been married. The fact that she was sexually pure was simply assumed. Today, the word *virgin* has a sexual connotation and may even be considered an impolite word to use in mixed company. We certainly would not want to refer to our daughters in a way that would stir improper thoughts of the state of their sexuality!

Discussing virginity in public or in mixed company throws some Christians into fits of pious mortification. Furthermore, "polite society" tells us we should pretend that those around us are not overdone and underdressed, when in fact many times they are. We are taught that *talking* about immodesty is shameful, but allowing it in our families and churches is not. Is it the word that is sinful . . . or the action?

Chastity is commanded in Scripture, to the virgin and married woman alike (Titus 2:5). It is different from abstinence or celibacy. A chaste maiden *is* a virgin, but being chaste is more than merely a physical state of being. It is an active virtue that consistently demonstrates purity—in thought, word, and deed. Along with the word *chastity*, we have forgotten the proper meaning of many other good words.

In our modern culture, girls tend to be referred to in a variety of ways. Some people simply use terms, such as "kids," "children," "teens," or "youth." Someone may occasionally ask, "How many *daughters* do you have?" but you will never hear anyone ask, "How many *virgins* do you have?" or "How many *maidens* are in your family?" Is it that our contemporary dictionaries don't have room for these outdat-

ed terms or is it that our culture embraces gender neutrality and spurns titles that signify innocence or purity?

To Whom Are You Referring, Sir?

In addition, unmarried young women are often referred to by young men as chicks, babes, or even *hotties*! Why aren't we shocked—why aren't young ladies insulted? Why aren't fathers and brothers grabbing their shotguns?

The Webster's 1828 Dictionary defines the word *maiden* as "a young unmarried woman; a virgin; fresh; new; unused." It goes on to describe a maiden as one who speaks and acts "demurely or modestly." I don't believe that the extinction of this term is accidental, but instead that it exposes a disturbing loss of virtue and dignity in modern womanhood.

In this study you will see the term *maiden* sprinkled liberally throughout the text. My goal isn't necessarily to resurrect an antiquated word, but to instill its meaning into the hearts and minds of young women. By becoming better acquainted with the definition and its significance, young ladies may come to a better understanding of the fundamental nature of maidenhood and embrace its personality.

Making a Purity Statement

As Christians, we must understand that Scripture teaches unmarried young women (and men) to remain pure until they are married. Our sons and daughters are to remain physically and spiritually faithful to their future spouses. Our daughters are to be protected—remaining under the authority of their fathers, untouched until the moment in which they are delivered, spotless and pure, to their husbands on their wedding day. Likewise, for those of us with sons, what a blessing it will be to offer a groom pure, strong, and honorable to his bride on that special day (Psalm 119:9).

The world's daughters are embarrassed and ashamed of virginity and make every effort to appear as far from that image as possible . . . and with navel rings, heavy makeup, tight clothing, and revealing or sheer tops, you have to admit most of them are doing a great job!

A wise and noble Christian maiden desires to bring honor to her earthly father as she glorifies her Heavenly One. In addition, she loves her brothers in Christ enough to show concern for their spiritual welfare. She does not walk or dress in a way that would compromise their (or her own) purity. She remains aware of her duty to remain true to her future husband, and is sensitive to the fact that any boy she meets is most likely someone *else's* future husband.

It is true that each man and boy is responsible to guard his own eyes (Job 31:1), but a virtuous maiden does not make it difficult for him. Unfortunately, many times we cannot see much difference between the daughters of the world and the daughters of the Living God. Scripture teaches us that as Believers, we are the Bride of Christ (Ephesians 5:31-32). Can you imagine the Lord Jesus Christ returning to a Bride who has purposely adorned herself in ripped, form-fitting jeans or short skirts; navel rings; immodest, sloppy tops; and heavy makeup?

And it shall come to pass, that instead of sweet smell there shall be stink; and instead of a girdle a rent; and instead of well set hair baldness; and instead of a stomacher a girding of sackcloth; and burning instead of beauty. (Isaiah 3:24)

Our world today assaults men of all ages. Everywhere they look they see indecently dressed women: on billboards, in pictures in department stores, on magazines in grocery-store checkout lanes, even walking down the street.

I recently picked up a bottle of hairspray at our local grocery store for my eighteen-year-old daughter, Tiffany. When she decided to use it the following Sunday, what she found on the back of the bottle shocked her, and she came downstairs to show me. This is what it said:

"WHAT YOU WEAR BEGINS WITH YOUR HAIR™ What's on your body. . . skin-tight jeans. What's in your hair...SHPRITZ FORTE® glam rock finishing spray for big, sexy, rock 'n roll hair. . ."

The verbiage became more graphic the further I read. I'll spare you the details. I didn't even know people paid attention to the backs of hairspray bottles. Obviously someone does.

When the lady who worked at the customer service counter asked our reason for returning the bottle of spray, we simply showed her the back of the bottle and told her we didn't *want* "big, sexy, rock 'n roll hair." Given the way she looked at us, I'm sure she wondered why we thought we were in any danger.

A Bride Adorned

As believers we are to take dominion of the world by using every area of our lives to glorify Him. We will not see reform in the Church until we see reform in our own lives and families. How can we show the world a pure and spotless Bride if the Bride looks, talks, and swaggers like a strumpet? We are to be set apart.

> *Ye are the salt of the earth: but if the salt have lost his savour, wherewith shall it be salted? it is thenceforth good for nothing, but to be cast out, and to be trodden under foot of men.* (Matthew 5:13)

As she prepares for her wedding, the Bride must put away, even burn, her attire of harlotry and allow her holy Groom to adorn her in spotless white robes of righteousness and dignity.

> *I will greatly rejoice in the LORD, my soul shall be joyful in my God; for he hath clothed me with the garments of salvation, he hath covered me with the robe of righteousness, as a bridegroom decketh himself with ornaments, and as a bride adorneth herself with her jewels. For as the earth bringeth forth her bud, and as the garden causeth the things that are sown in it to spring forth; so the Lord GOD will cause righteousness and praise to spring forth before all the nations.* (Isaiah 61:10-11)

The Beauty of the Lord

A godly young maiden considers her demeanor, making sure her deportment declares feminine wholesomeness as opposed to genderless sloppiness or sensual tarnish. A wise maiden ignores the lies of modern music and media and pays no attention to the fleeting whims of professional marketers and Hollywood. Instead, she continually meditates on the timeless truths of Scripture, presenting to the watching world a picture of purity and loveliness that honestly displays the goodness and beauty of a holy God.

> *And let the beauty of the LORD our God be upon us: and establish thou the work of our hands upon us; yea, the work of our hands establish thou it.* (Psalm 90:17)

It is a Christian daughter's *duty* to reflect purity—literally. She has an obligation to be a symbol of *virginity* when she walks into a room. Why would a Christian young lady desire to masquerade as someone else—as someone who is impure? To do so would be to lie about the very nature of Christ. A modest young maiden makes more than a fashion statement—she makes a *purity* statement!

> *A garden enclosed is my sister, my spouse; a spring shut up, a fountain sealed.* (Song of Solomon 4:12)

Share Your Heart

- ✎ If you are in public and see a girl who is dressed in boyish clothing or carries herself in a masculine way, which of the following thoughts might come to mind?
  - What a lovely young lady! She must be a Christian.
  - Is that a boy or a girl?
  - I wouldn't want to make *her* mad!
- ✎ If you are in public and see a girl who is dressed immodestly, which

of the following thoughts come to mind?

- What a lovely young lady! She must be a Christian.
- How sad, she must not have any respect for herself.
- Maybe she doesn't realize her undergarments are showing—I should probably tell her before she embarrasses herself further.

❧ What about when you see a young woman who is dressed modestly, in a neat and clean dress, and speaking in a gentle, respectful, and kind way? Might you wonder if *she* is a Christian? Why? Discuss with your mother the importance of communicating Christ to others with your deportment.

❧ How can you be sure that people automatically know you are a girl when they see you from a distance (without revealing or accentuating your private feminine parts)?

❧ When *you* walk into a room, do you think people view you as a virgin-like maiden? Why or why not?

❧ Have people whom you have never met ever asked you if you were a Christian, simply from observing your appearance and behavior?

❧ Look up the word *tough* in the dictionary. Now look up the word *strong*. Ask five good friends which word describes you best. Discuss with your mother the difference between being tough and being strong.

❧ Are you pleased with the way you are perceived by others? Why or why not?

❧ How do you think the way you dress, speak, treat others, and carry yourself reflects upon your father? Your family? Your Heavenly Father? (1 Timothy 2:9-10)

❧ What do you think it means to make a purity statement? What are some practical ways to do this?

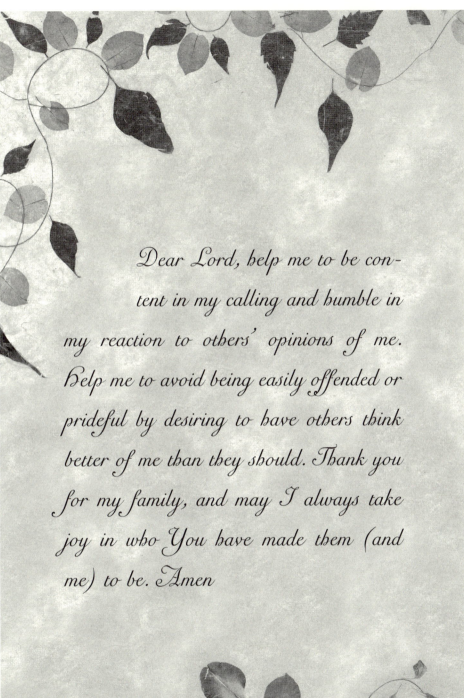

Dear Lord, help me to be content in my calling and humble in my reaction to others' opinions of me. Help me to avoid being easily offended or prideful by desiring to have others think better of me than they should. Thank you for my family, and may I always take joy in who You have made them (and me) to be. Amen

Chapter 3

A NOBLE CALLING

Excerpted from: *From Dark to Dawn: A Tale of Martin Luther and the Reformation* by Elizabeth Rundle Charles (originally published as *Chronicles of the Schönberg-Cotta Family*, 1862; reprint, Books on the Path, 2003)

In this story, we peer into the heart of Agnes, a young girl who lived in Germany during the time of the Reformation. Just like all of us, she struggles with issues of pride and contentment. Read the following excerpt aloud and discuss the topics at the end of this chapter.

To me it always seemed, and seems still, that nothing can be nobler than our dear father's office of telling the people the way to Heaven on Sundays, and teaching their children the way to be wise and good on earth in the week. It was a shock to me when I found every one did not think the same.

Not that every one was not always most kind to me, but it happened in this way.

One day some visitors had been at Uncle Ulrich's castle. They had complimented me on my golden hair, which Heinz always says is the color of the princess's in the fairy tale. I went out at Aunt Chriemhild's desire, feeling half shy and half flattered, to play with my cousins in the forest. As I was sitting hidden among the trees, twining wreaths from the forget-me-nots my cousins were gathering by the stream below, these ladies passed again. I heard one of them say, "Yes, she is a well-mannered little thing for a schoolmaster's daughter."

"I cannot think where a burgher maid—the Cottas are all burghers, are they not?—should inherit those little white hands and those delicate features," said the other.

"Poor, too, doubtless, as they must be!" was the reply. "One would think she had never had to work about the house, as no doubt she must."

"Who was her grandfather?"

"Only a printer at Wittenberg!"

"Only a schoolmaster!" and "only a printer!" My whole heart was against the scornful words. Was this what people meant by paying compliments? Was this the estimate my father was held in the world—he, the noblest man in it, who was fit to be the Elector or the Emperor? A bitter feeling came over me, which I thought was affection and an aggrieved sense of justice. But love is scarcely so bitter, or justice so fiery.

I did not tell anyone, nor did I shed a tear, but went on weaving my forget-me-not wreaths, and forswore the wicked and hollow world.

At Aunt Else's, however, another experience awaited me. There was to be a fair, and we were all to go in our best holiday dresses. My cousins had rich oriental jewels on their bodices; and although, as burgher maidens, they might not, like my cousins at the castle, wear velvets, they had jackets and dresses of the stiffest, richest silks which Uncle Reichenbach had sent for from Italy and the East.

My stuff dress certainly looked plain beside them, but I did not care in the least for that; my own dear mother and I had made it together; and she had hunted up some old precious stores to make me a taffeta jacket, which, as it was the most magnificent apparel I had ever possessed, we had both looked at it with much complacency. Nor did it seem to me in the least less beautiful now. The touch of my mother's fingers had been on it, as she smoothed it round me the evening before I came away.

And Aunt Else had said it was exactly like my mother. But my cousins were not quite pleased, it was evident—especially Fritz and the elder boys. They said nothing; but on the morning of the fete, a beautiful new dress— the counterpart of my cousin's—was laid at my bedside before I awoke.

I put it on with some pleasure, but when I looked at myself in the glass—it was very unreasonable—I could not bear it. It seemed a reproach on my mother, and on my humble life and my dear, poor home at Eisleben, and I sat down and cried bitterly, until a gentle knock at the door aroused me; and Aunt Else came in, and found me sitting with tears on my face and on the beautiful new dress, exceedingly ashamed of myself.

"Don't you like it, my child? It was Fritz's thought. I was afraid you might not be pleased."

"My mother thought the old one good enough," I said in a very faltering tone. "It was good enough for my home. I had better go home again."

Aunt Else was carefully wiping away the tears from my dress, but at these words she began to cry herself, and drew me to her heart, and said it was exactly what she should have felt in her young days at Eisenach, but that I must just wear the new dress to the fete, and then I need never wear it again unless I liked; and that I was right in thinking nothing half so good as my mother, and all she did, because nothing ever was, or would be, she was sure.

So we cried together, and were comforted; and I wore the green taffeta to the fair.

But when I came home again to Eisleben, I felt more ashamed of myself than of the taffeta dress or of the flattering ladies at the Castle. The dear, precious old home, in spite of all I could persuade myself to the contrary, did look small and poor, and the furniture worn and old. And yet I could see there new traces of care and welcome everywhere—fresh rushes on the floors; a plain new quilt on my little bed, made, I knew, by my mother's hands.

She knew very soon that I was feeling troubled about something, and soon she knew it all, as I told her my bitter experiences of life.

"Your father 'only a schoolmaster'!" she said, "and you yourself presented with a new taffeta dress! Are these all your grievances, little Agnes?"

"All, Mother," I exclaimed, "and only!"

"Is your father anything else but a schoolmaster, Agnes?" she said.

"I am not ashamed of that for an instant, Mother," I said; "you could not think it. I think it is much nobler to teach children than to hunt foxes, and buy and sell bales of silk and wool. But the world seems to me exceedingly hollow and crooked; and I never wish to see any more of it. Oh, Mother do you think it was all nonsense in me?"

"I think, my child, you have had an encounter with the world, the flesh, and the devil; and I think they are no contemptible enemies. And I think you have not left them behind."

"But is not our father's calling nobler than any one's, and our home the nicest in the world?" I said; "and Eisleben really as beautiful in its way as the Thuringian Forest, and as wise as Wittenberg?"

"All callings may be noble," she said; "and the one God calls us to is the noblest for us. Eisleben is not, I think, as beautiful as the old forest-covered hills at Gersdorf; nor Luther's birthplace as great as his dwelling place, where he preaches and teaches, and sheds around him the influence of his holy daily life. Other homes may be as good as yours, dear child, though none can be so to you."

And so I learned that what makes any calling noble is its being commanded by God, and what makes anything good is its being given by God; and that honest contentment consists not in persuading ourselves that our things are the very best in the world, but in believing they are the best for us, and giving God thanks for them.

Share Your Heart

Read the following quote from our story:

"A bitter feeling came over me, which I thought was affection and an aggrieved sense of justice. But love is scarcely so bitter, or justice so fiery."

❧ What do you think Agnes meant by this? What do you think was the real reason this young maiden experienced bitterness when she overheard the women gossiping in the woods?

❧ Why did Agnes's mother say that she thought her daughter had "not left the world and the devil behind" that day?

❧ Have you ever been hurt by the careless or insensitive words of others? Share an example. How did you react? Did you let bitterness overtake you?

❧ What made Agnes's old dress special to her?

❧ When she came home again to Eisleben, why did she feel even more ashamed of herself than before?

❧ List the following vocations in order of importance:
- Doctor
- President
- Mother
- Theologian
- Missionary
- Father

❧ Were you able to complete this task? *Are* some vocations "more important" than others? What makes a calling noble? Discuss your answer, using Scripture to back up your reasons.

❧ Have you ever felt ashamed of your family for any reason? Discuss your answer, examining whether or not your reasons were scripturally legitimate.

❧ Agnes realizes that her bitterness was the result of an ungodly reaction to the opinions of others. With help from her mother, she gains some interesting nuggets of wisdom. What did Agnes learn was the *secret* to her contentment?

❧ What about you? Are you harboring any bitterness against someone who has spoken ill of you or of someone you love? Have *you* "left the world and the devil behind?" Take this time to pray and discuss your answers.

Lord, help me to set aside my shortsighted goals and desires and honestly seek Your will. Train my heart for contentment and guard it from the temptations of busy living. Give me a love and passion for home life and a genuine trust in my parents' leadership. Help me to obey Your Word so that I might glorify and enjoy You forever. Amen.

Chapter 4

HOMEMADE HOMEMAKERS:

Becoming a Home-Centered Maiden

That they may teach the young women to be sober, to love their husbands, to love their children, To be discreet, chaste, keepers at home, good, obedient to their own husbands, that the word of God be not blasphemed. (Titus 2:4-5)

T he grass was tall and wispy and the field of delicate wildflowers blew in the wind like a wild blanket of unleashed color dancing to some secret tune. Bethany pushed her carriage and gently cradled her precious doll as she wandered the familiar path with her mother to the local country store.

Mrs. Stewart was inside the market doing her weekly shopping when she spotted Bethany and her mother entering the store pushing Bethany's bulky pram. Mrs. Stewart pushed her jeweled glasses up on her nose and decided this was her opportunity to ask this peculiar family a few questions.

She politely said hello to Bethany's mother and then quickly turned her attention to the "Little Mother" who was humming softly to her doll.

"What do you want to be when you grow up?" she asked Bethany.

Bethany smiled and looked affectionately at her mama. "I want to get married, be a mommy, and have lots of babies."

The lady with the funny glasses wrinkled her nose and looked irritated. "Yes, you may choose to marry and have a baby . . . or so, but what do you want to *be*?" Glancing at Bethany's mother impatiently, the inquisitor added, "After *College*?"

Changing her manner to a more persuasive and gentle tone, she went on question-ing the little girl, "Don't you know you can be *anything* you want—an astronaut, a doctor, a soldier—what do you want to *be?*"

Busily, Bethany tucked her baby doll into her carriage and lovingly patted the handmade doll blanket. She looked puzzled and asked curiously, "Can they teach me how to be a good mommy in college?"

Bethany's mother smiled and took her little girl by the hand. "No," she inter-jected. "That's my job."

———◆———

If you have been raised to love God and respect His plan for families, then you almost certainly dream of some day marrying a godly husband who loves and pro-tects you. You also probably hope for plenty of babies to rock and cuddle. If you have been raised by parents with a generational vision, you may plan to home-school and faithfully train your own children in the ways of God night and day (Deuteronomy 6:7-9).

Yet not everyone will be called to marriage. We all know godly Christians who never married. So what if you are going to be single your whole life? Shouldn't you prepare for that day? Shouldn't you go to college in case you ever *have* to work? Shouldn't you get a part-time job somewhere to become independent and gain some experience in the workforce? Before we go further, let us consider whether singleness or marriage is normative in Scripture.

What are the purposes of marriage?

- ✤ Marriage is a picture of Christ and His Church (Ephesians 5:25-27, 32).
- ✤ Marriage is the tool used to raise up godly seed (generations of Christian children) for His kingdom (Genesis12:1-3, Psalm 128:6).
- ✤ Husbands and wives are to take dominion of the earth together (occupy, influence, control, dominate), (Genesis 1:28).

Whoso findeth a wife findeth a good thing, and obtaineth favour of the LORD.
(Proverbs 18:22)

Here in Proverbs, the book of wisdom, we find that marriage between a godly man and woman is a *good* thing. We also see that it brings favor from the Lord.

Who can find a virtuous woman? for her price is far above rubies. The heart of her husband doth safely trust in her, so that he shall have no need of spoil. She will do him good and not evil all the days of her life. (Proverbs 31:10-12)

Here a young man is instructed in what to look for in a wife. He is told how *rare and precious* a good wife truly is and what sort of wife will bring him good and not evil all the days of her life: a virtuous wife—a hard-to-find jewel. A good wife will be his helpmate as he serves God and takes dominion over the earth.

Where do good wives come from? They don't just happen—good wives are either trained to be successful wives and mothers . . . or they are not. If you are a Christian maiden and plan to be a wife and mother, shouldn't you be working alongside your mother, focusing together on your goal of becoming this rare and precious jewel?

Thy wife shall be as a fruitful vine by the sides of thine house: thy children like olive plants round about thy table. Behold, that thus shall the man be blessed that feareth the LORD. . .Yea, thou shalt see thy children's children, and peace upon Israel.
(Psalm 128:3-4, 6)

Here again, we see the blessing of a godly marriage resulting in the expansion of a godly family—a blessed man training up sanctified seed for the Lord.

We might expect that Scripture would instruct younger women to find a trade or a means of making an independent living. Wouldn't this appear to be wise advice? Isn't that what most people say young ladies should do—prepare to be breadwinners, *just in case?*

Timothy had different instructions for young maidens:

I will therefore that the younger women marry, bear children, guide the house, give none occasion to the adversary to speak reproachfully. (1 Timothy 5:14)

Notice that instead of instructing younger women to find specialized training or learn a trade, he encourages them to marry, bear children, and guide the house. Older women are not instructed to assist young women in finding a fulfilling career or ministry, but to be keepers at home, obedient to their husbands, and loving to their children.

So if singleness is not the Scriptural norm, and marriage and being a keeper at home is, doesn't it seem logical that marriage and homemaking should be our focus of training?

If we want to train to do something well, we train for what we expect we will actually be doing. If a Christian man wants to be an engineer, we don't see him running off to auto-mechanic school *just in case* he is ever laid off. He trains diligently for the desired result and trusts that God will equip him for any emergencies that might arise. Women who train to be breadwinners can expect to be very good breadwinners, but not necessarily very good bread*makers* . . . or homemakers.

I often hear from women who were never taught to cook when they were young. Many genuinely struggle with organizing and cleaning their homes consistently, mastering basic cooking skills, and being content at home with children all day. What is even more interesting is that most of these frustrated women are college graduates.

Some are accomplished career women, yet many gave birth to their first child without ever having changed a diaper. In fact, many hospitals now have mandatory diaper-changing classes which parents must attend before they are *allowed* to take their newborn infants home. Before marriage, most of these women knew how to drive a car, balance a checkbook, change a tire, and even run a cash register; yet they were unprepared for keeping a home, helping a husband, and nurturing children—the very purposes for their design.

A young maiden should be well-trained, well-spoken, well-educated, and thoroughly prepared for her future life as a Christian woman who is ready, willing, and able to make an impact on a humanistic culture at war with God. Her education should be focused on assisting her future husband as his valuable helpmate, not on becoming her "own person." This is where true reform in the family and ultimately in the church will be born.

You, young maidens, are the mothers of the future. You have the ability to impact generations for Christ. Although a college degree may be a fine personal goal, our intellect and education should be used for God's glory, not our own. We should not be selfish with what God has given us, because all good qualities are gifts from Him to use as He wishes, but we must be certain that our goals and aspirations line up with the Word of God.

Share Your Heart

- ✎ What are your strengths? What gifts has God given you? Ask your parents to help you make a list of your natural skills and talents.

- ✎ Who does God's Word say is the head of the family? (1 Corinthians 11:3, Ephesians 5:22-24, Ephesians 6:1-3, Colossians 3:18, Hebrews 13:17). How does this affect you?

- ✎ What are some ways you can develop your mind while you honor and serve your father at home? Discuss the following ideas for serving others while you grow spiritually and prepare for your likely future as a wife and mother:
  - Help in the family home business or ministry
  - Take correspondence or online courses
  - Help homeschool siblings
  - Tutor homeschoolers

- Offer music, sewing, or other lessons to children
- Develop fine arts skills
- Study theology or pursue higher education
- Develop writing skills
- Pursue expertise in gardening, cooking, baking, or arts and crafts
- Care for a sick relative or friend
- Assist overwhelmed mothers

ᔾ Ask God to make you willing to set aside your own goals and desires if they do not line up with God's will. Remember that a strong desire to be a doctor or a seemingly God-given talent in math is not an indication of God's will for you to have a career in medicine or engineering. Sometimes God gives us talents and strengths for the specific purpose of helping our future husbands in their calling. Pray that He will give your parents wisdom in training you for the task He has planned for you.

ᔾ Ask God how you might best ready yourself so that your gifts and talents would bring the greatest glory and honor to His name. Ask Him to make you diligent in studying and preparing for your future.

ᔾ Read Genesis 34:1-5 and study the following commentary on these verses.

She is reckoned now but fifteen or sixteen years of age when she here occasioned so much mischief. Observe her vain curiosity, which exposed her. She went out, perhaps unknown to her father, but by the connivance of her mother, to see the daughters of the land (v. 1); probably it was at a ball, or on some public day. Being an only daughter, she thought herself solitary at home, having none of her own age and sex to converse with; and therefore she must need to go abroad to divert herself, to keep off melancholy, and to accomplish herself by conversation better than she could in her father's tents. . .

It is a very good thing for children to love home; it is parents' wisdom to make it easy to them, and children's duty then to be easy in it...

See what came of Dinah's gadding: young women must learn to be chaste, keepers at home; these properties are put together, Titus 2:5, for those that are not keepers at home expose their chastity. Dinah went abroad to look about her; but, if she had looked about her as she ought, she would not have fallen into this snare. Note, The beginning of sin is as the letting forth of water. (*Matthew Henry's Commentary on the Whole Bible,* New Modern Edition, Complete and Unabridged; Hendrickson Publishers, Inc., 1991, p. 160)

ॐ How could leaving the protection of your father's house for reasons other than marriage result in a dangerous or ungodly situation? What about college, mission trips, or youth functions?

ॐ Make a "Maiden Days Reading List" of books that you wish to read this year. Ask your mother to help you choose books that will complement your natural skills and interests and books that are "must-reads" for preparing for motherhood or for being a godly wife. Be sure to refer to the reading list in the back of this book

Dear Lord, help me to love my family the way that You love me. Help me to experience Your joy in every seemingly mundane task I perform. Let me be a blessing to my parents and siblings as I serve You through loving and serving them. Teach me, O Lord, that I might learn Your ways and not the ways of the world. Make me a willing vessel of shining gold, as You purge the dross from my life. Grant me contentment as I learn to submit peacefully to Your transforming hand. Amen.

Chapter 5

LOVING YOUR OWN NEST

But godliness with contentment is great gain. (1 Timothy 6:6)

A family that includes nine children, a homeschool, and a home business makes for some hectic days. Because of this, our older daughters have been a particular blessing to our busy family. My husband and I are well aware, however, that we live in a society that usually views large families like ours as an oddity rather than a blessing.

We teach our children that it is an honor and a privilege to serve one another, but there are well-meaning folks who ask our children annoying questions like, "So what do you do for *fun?*" "You mean you spend your weekends with your *family?*" "You mean you *like* being around your brothers and sisters?" Since we require more from our children than the average modern parent expects, it is not surprising when restlessness and discontent attempt to enter into the hearts of our children.

My second oldest daughter, Tiffany, shares the following experience of her own struggle with contentment:

> There was a time when I found myself wishing for a life God had not chosen for me. One night, when the house was quiet, I snuggled beneath

my warm, thick comforter and began to reflect upon recent days.

I quietly remembered visiting some friends in their home. They have three children who have graduated from high school and no longer have babies to watch and messes to clean. I recall envy filling my heart as I looked around their house and noticed that their living room was spotless. There were no puzzle pieces under the coffee table waiting to be put back where they belong. They didn't have mud stains on the carpet by the door from little feet, or coffee stains by the counter from chubby fingers reaching for a good sip of sweetened coffee and cream—and no dirty diapers to change! Their time seemed to be their own. I imagined relaxing on the couch with a good book and no noisy toddlers running about. I envisioned eating a piece of cake without a four-year-old climbing in my lap asking for a bite. Peace! Why couldn't *our* family be that way?

Discontentment began to creep in and take dominion over my life. Every day I would find some other fault with our family, some other reason to be jealous. My every thought seemed to begin with, "If only our family. . ."

The babies began to become burdensome to me; they were no longer a joy to be around. It seemed that each day brought more messes and even more laundry to fold and put away. I thought it was the babies who were being grumpy, when in reality, it was I.

Then this verse in Scripture struck me squarely in the head: *Lo, children are an heritage of the LORD: and the fruit of the womb is his reward. As arrows are in the hand of a mighty man; so are children of the youth.* (Psalm 127:3-4)

I began to think about what our family would be like without the four youngest children. Sure, the house would be cleaner, but would that really matter to me if I had to sacrifice my sweet little brother and sisters for a clean house?

The discontented spirit had begun to weigh me down. I had been cross, mean, and miserable. When I could bear it no longer, I finally called on the Lord to bring me out of the "miry pit." I asked Him to set my feet on a "firm foundation," which reminded me of one of my favorite hymns. The fourth verse in "How Firm a Foundation" has encouraged me often. It reads:

When through fiery trials thy pathway shall lie,
My grace, all-sufficient, shall be thy supply;
The flame shall not hurt thee, I only design
Thy dross to consume, and thy gold to refine.

God is sovereign, and though *we* don't always know what His plan is or why, *He* has known since before the foundations of the world.

When He brings you through "fiery trials," trust Him; pray for His all-sufficient grace. Be content with where He has you, for *There hath no temptation taken you but such as is common to man: but God is faithful, who will not suffer you to be tempted above that ye are able; but will with the temptation also make a way to escape, that ye may be able to bear it.* (1 Corinthians 10:13)

Ask Him to give you strength—the strength and peace that come from none but Him. As the hymn so powerfully states, "His flame shall not hurt you." He is bringing you through this trial to consume your dross (impurity) and to refine your gold. Instead of falling into discontent, seek God; realize that this is all part of His plan for you and that it is for His ultimate purpose and glory. Allow Him—no, *ask* Him—to consume your dross, get rid of all the junk in your heart, and *refine* your gold until it shines and glistens with the purity and goodness of a true maiden of virtue and worth! *The king's daughter is all glorious within: her clothing is of wrought gold* (Psalm 45:13).

As I sit back and review my journey, I realize that when I am content, a peaceful spirit covers me, and life seems to run smoothly, even if things aren't going my way. The complete opposite happens when I keep my eyes on what others have or dwell on what I think I *should* have. As I enter into each new season of life, I pray that God will remind me of the lessons I have learned, and that I will always remember that He is sovereign and that His plan is flawless.

Share Your Heart

- Do you ever wish you were part of another family instead of your own or wonder if other daughters have it easier or better than you do? How could this type of thinking be a rejection of God's sovereign will—and ultimately rebellion against God?

- Which commandment are you breaking when you look at another family and long for the life they live? If you have been guilty of this, stop right now and repent. Pray that God would forgive you and give you a thankful spirit for what He has given you. Pray that you will learn from your imperfect family all that God wants to teach you.

- List five things about your own family that remind you of your love for them. Thank God aloud for these things.

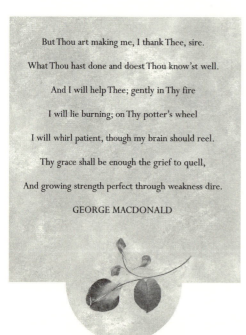

But Thou art making me, I thank Thee, sire.

What Thou hast done and doest Thou know'st well.

And I will help Thee; gently in Thy fire

I will lie burning; on Thy potter's wheel

I will whirl patient, though my brain should reel.

Thy grace shall be enough the grief to quell,

And growing strength perfect through weakness dire.

GEORGE MACDONALD

- Pray for your father's leadership and wisdom and that God would give your mother strength, encouragement, and discernment.

- Acknowledge and thank God for using each member of your family to care for you and help you to grow.

- Write a letter to your father thanking him for His

love for you and your siblings and his special love for your mother. Let him know that you appreciate the sacrifices he has made and thank him for protecting and leading your family.

ᵝ Purpose to choose a different family member each day to pray for specifically, and deliberately show your love for him or her in some act of service.

Dear Lord, give me eyes to see and ears to hear. Help me to recognize the shallow façade of the unrighteous. Forgive me for the moments when I covet the lives of those who are perishing, and give me a hunger and thirst for life—true life. Give me a godly desire to please my earthly father as I glorify You, my heavenly Father. Amen.

DADDY'S FAIR MAIDEN

But ye are a chosen generation, a royal priesthood, an holy nation, a peculiar-people; that ye should shew forth the praises of him who hath called you out of darkness into his marvellous light. (1 Peter 2:9)

*E*mily waited for her parents by the water fountain, the designated meeting place, after Sunday school class was over. She watched the young people file out of the classroom. Many, she knew, did not claim Christ, though they came to church and Sunday school each week—a prerequisite for attending Friday night youth group. Youth group—this was one of seemingly many activities she wasn't allowed to join. Emily tried to shrug off the growing sense of resentment. Why did her family always have to be so different?

Emily's parents had asked her if she would join them in their adult Sunday school class so they could all learn together. She already attended the worship service with her parents—instead of sitting with the "youth kids." Emily had begged to remain in the teen Sunday school class at least until the end of the year, and her father had reluctantly agreed. All the other kids at church were in age-segregated classrooms—she didn't want to be different *again*.

Loud, obnoxious girls walked by laughing. One girl turned and looked at Emily with a smirk. The girl blew a bubble and let it pop almost in Emily's face. Emily's eyes burned with threatened tears as she looked at the floor. She heard a few boys laugh. Suddenly she felt very conspicuous and out of place here—at church. Why couldn't she be like everyone else? Why couldn't she enjoy friends and peer approval like other girls? (1 Corinthians 5:11)

Although Emily had many good friends, at the moment it seemed as though she didn't have a friend in the world. Confused by her mixed desire to fit in, she temporarily lost sight of the wonderful family life she had. For a moment, she even forgot God.

She tried in vain to shut out the Word of God that rang in her heart: *How can ye believe, which receive honour one of another, and seek not the honour that cometh from God only?"* (John 5:44)

Against her will, she found herself admiring the clothing of these worldly, older girls who swaggered by. Secretly she imagined herself talking to boys with the same smooth-tongued confidence she saw in Brittney, a pretty sixteen-year-old girl who had started attending Emily's Sunday school class last month.

She knew Brittney's dress and behavior did not honor God, yet Emily found herself drawn to her magnetic personality and even a little jealous of her sophisticated appearance.

Emily looked down at the simple, pretty dress she was wearing. Her mother had made it for her last summer, and Emily had relished the time spent alone with her helping to sew on the lace trim and silk buttons. She had thought it the most beautiful dress she had ever seen and had twirled around as fast as she could to make the skirt form a circle in the air. Somehow, she now felt strange and conspicuous in her beautiful dress—maybe even a little silly.

Brittney sashayed past Emily with an entourage of admiring boys. Emily wondered what it felt like to have boys look at her the way they looked at Brittney. She blushed as she imagined dressing in Brittney's clothes and enjoying the same attention from boys. She knew Brittney dated; she pondered what it was like.

Her thoughts suddenly switched to her father and how disappointed he would be with her recent thoughts. She found herself feeling ashamed and confused.

Emily had felt secure and protected the day her father had taken her hands in his and promised to protect her until the day he placed her hand in that of her hus-

band. She had agreed not to give her heart away, but instead to remain emotionally and physically pure before marriage, and to trust her parents' guidance through
courtship instead of dating (Isaiah 62:5).

"Where's my fair maiden?" asked a strong, loving voice behind her. Emily
snapped out of her reverie of discontent and faced her protector ashamed. He
stood beside her mother, his admiring eyes and cheerful words reminding her of
who she truly wanted to be—her father's fair maiden.

Then another thought hit her. What if she *were* to dress and act like Brittney?
Not only would she not be able to bear the disapproving gaze of her father, but
what would her future husband think of her? Would he turn and run? Would he
want to marry someone who behaved like a loose, silly girl, or would he be waiting for a true maiden of honor—as her father had done. Emily glanced tenderly at
her mother.

In stark contrast, she turned to see Brittney hanging on a boy's arm laughing
indiscreetly. She contemplated further: if he were interested in someone like
Brittney, would Emily really want to marry *him*—a man with no depth, no standards or wisdom, led only by his visual, temporal pleasures? No way!

Then, worst of all, she thought of Jesus. He didn't have to wait for her words
or actions—He read her thoughts. He knew she had been coveting things that
were not meant for her—or any other daughter of the King.

> That every one of you should know how to possess his vessel in sanctification and
> honour; Not in the lust of concupiscence, even as the Gentiles which know not God:
> That no man go beyond and defraud his brother in any matter: because that the
> Lord is the avenger of all such, as we also have forewarned you and testified. For
> God hath not called us unto uncleanness, but unto holiness. He therefore that
> despiseth, despiseth not man, but God, who hath also given unto us his holy Spirit.
> (1 Thessalonians 4:4-8)

Right then and there Emily confessed her sinful desires to the Lord and repented. Again, she remembered her father's words, "Where's my fair maiden?" A lump formed in her throat and she threw her arms around her surprised father. "Here I am, Daddy!" Emily knew, beyond a shadow of a doubt, who she wanted to be.

> Who can find a virtuous woman? for her price is far above rubies.
> (Proverbs 31:10)

Emily didn't notice, but Brittney had caught sight of the precious father-daughter embrace, and a curious pang of longing struck her heart. What was it like to be loved and protected the way this young girl was loved and protected? How must it feel to be so confident in *God's* love that you didn't have to beg for the wrong kind of attention by stooping to flirtatious stunts? Emily was the only girl at church who had appeared different to Brittney.

Emily had always been respectful to the adults in class, and Brittney had marveled at how Emily had controlled herself when Lisa rudely popped a bubble right in her face. Brittney considered the crude way she herself would have responded to the offense and felt convicted.

When she had first seen the way Emily dressed, Brittney had laughed, wondering what 1950s movie the girl had stepped out of. Later Brittney began to feel a little envious. Emily always looked so feminine and seemed to carry herself with such an air of . . . dignity.

Brittney had met many Christians at this church, but she hadn't met any who seemed to be much different than anyone else she knew. Maybe this Emily and her family really were different—maybe they actually had some answers. She decided to ask (Matthew 5:13-16).

———————

Remember, you are a Christian maiden—a daughter of the King. If you imitate the behavior or fashion statements of the daughters of the world, then how are they to know what a Christian maiden is and how she should carry herself?

Many Christian maidens are duped into following the crowd—being pulled around by an imaginary leash at the whim of a perverse and death-loving culture.

You can show the world what it means to be a daughter of virtue by obeying God and honoring your father and mother in the way you present yourself to others. As you reject the ways of the world, the grace of God will help you embrace a life that is above reproach. By your very presence in a room you will bring glory and honor to the name of Christ!

Share Your Heart

Give unto the LORD the glory due unto his name; worship the LORD in the beauty of holiness. (Psalm 29:2)

- Read aloud Psalm 29:2. One reason a young maiden may desire to resemble the world is from a mixed-up understanding of true beauty. Think about the meaning of the "beauty of holiness" and discuss it with your mother.

- Read 1 Timothy 2:9-10. What sort of adornment would have made Brittney truly beautiful?

- Read Proverbs 11:22 and Proverbs 31:30. Have you ever secretly wished you could be like someone whom you viewed as beautiful—who seemed confident and popular, even though you knew she was not an example of godly maidenhood? After discussing true beauty, do you still think she is beautiful? Why or why not?

- Read 1 Corinthians 15:33. What changes might have occurred in Emily's personality and dress if she had befriended this particular group of young people?

- What kind of boys do you think would be attracted to Brittney? Do you think they would make faithful husbands? Would they be good fathers?

༄ What do you think the boys in our story really thought of Brittney? Do you think they would have wanted her for a wife? Would they want her to be the mother of their children? Why or why not?

༄ Why did Brittney suspect that Emily and her family might have the "answers" she was looking for?

༄ If Brittney were actually to approach Emily and ask about her relationship with her father, how could Emily explain virtuous maidenhood?

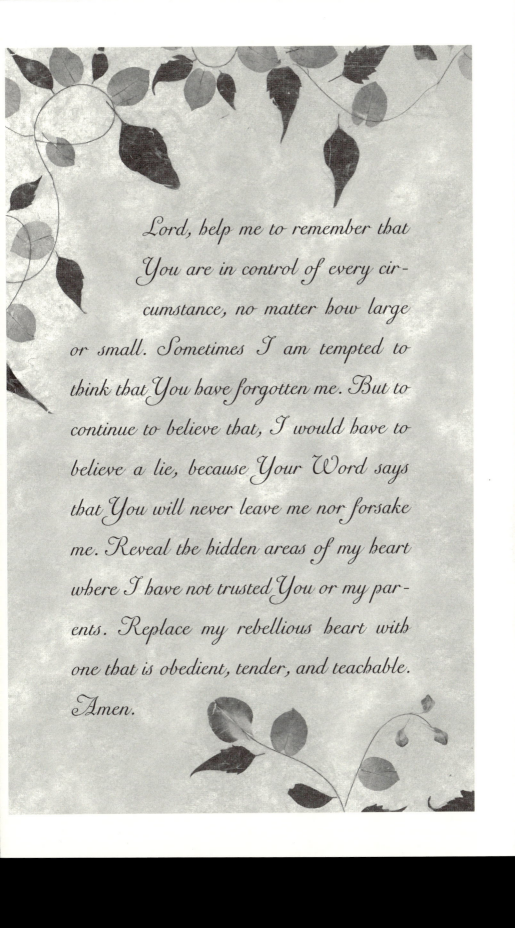

Lord, help me to remember that You are in control of every circumstance, no matter how large or small. Sometimes I am tempted to think that You have forgotten me. But to continue to believe that, I would have to believe a lie, because Your Word says that You will never leave me nor forsake me. Reveal the hidden areas of my heart where I have not trusted You or my parents. Replace my rebellious heart with one that is obedient, tender, and teachable. Amen.

Chapter 7

FRESH MILK

For I know the thoughts that I think toward you, saith the LORD, thoughts of peace, and not of evil, to give you an expected end. (Jeremiah 29:11)

annah had always wanted to live in the country, yet when her father quit his job and announced to the family that they were moving to Tennessee *and* that they were to live on a farm, she hardly knew what to think. At first she thought her prayers had been answered. Finally, she was going to taste fresh milk and raise chickens. No more neighborhood living for her! She was finally going to be free to breathe the fresh air and gather bouquets of wildflowers in the spring. She wondered if people who live in the country really walk barefoot through clear running streams like they do in the books she had read.

So if this was a dream come true, why did she feel so restless? She snuggled deep under her warm covers and tried to ignore the fleeting feelings of fear and discontent that disturbed her. What about her friend, Rose? Would she ever see their family again? She looked around the walls of her room—this was the only home she had ever known. What would it be like living somewhere else? What if she never had another friend again as long as she lived? Were there spiders and snakes in the country?

She began to wonder what her father was thinking—quitting his job like that!

She had noticed the concerned expression on her mother's face as he made the announcement to the family. Hannah considered the thought of her father having made a mistake. Surely her mother would never have said she thought so in front of the children. Maybe her father had made a rash decision and was stepping outside of God's will. Was that possible? What if Papa was leading the whole family into a desperate situation? The cold hand of fear and doubt gripped her heart. Her peace melted along with her trust and contentment.

Hannah couldn't stand the hopeless feeling a minute more. She threw back her covers and headed downstairs to ask her parents to pray for her. As she quietly walked down the hall, she noticed a dim light coming from the parlor. She heard whispering as she crept down the stairs. Quietly she looked around the corner and found her parents praying and thanking God. Hannah heard her mother's broken voice asking forgiveness for doubting God's sovereignty and trusting the riches of a secular job more than the riches of God's provision.

Hannah watched as her father raised his hands to Heaven, thanking God for his family. She listened as he asked for God to forgive his sins and as he prayed fervently for God's direction. Hannah's father beseeched God for his beloved bride and for each of their children.

Hannah's eyes burned with tears as she heard her father's strong yet tender voice pray specifically for her. She listened as he petitioned God for her own peace, protection, and contentment. God had not forgotten her. He was in control of even this. Hannah felt more love for her father and more trust in God than she had ever known (Hebrews 13:5-7, Romans 8:27-28).

Hannah knew those earlier doubts didn't matter now. God had called Hannah's family to live elsewhere; and she would trust Him, trust her father, and be content with His choice. She knew from Scripture that God orchestrates our lives and that His plans are good—and that Daddy was praying. Hannah hurried back to bed and snuggled deep under the handmade quilt she loved. Then she closed her eyes and tried to imagine the taste of fresh milk.

Share Your Heart

- ❧ Have you ever had mixed emotions about a major change in your family, such as a move, a new sibling, or a death? Share how God worked in your life.

- ❧ When you are frightened or unsure, do you ask your parents to pray for you? Why or why not?

- ❧ Do you trust your father? What if he was making a decision you thought was risky?

- ❧ Do you truly believe that God works through the decisions of your father, good or bad? Describe why or why not.

- ❧ Have you ever dreamed of living somewhere else? Explain your reasons.

- ❧ Do you believe God has you in the place you are now for a reason? If so, tell what has happened that makes it evident.

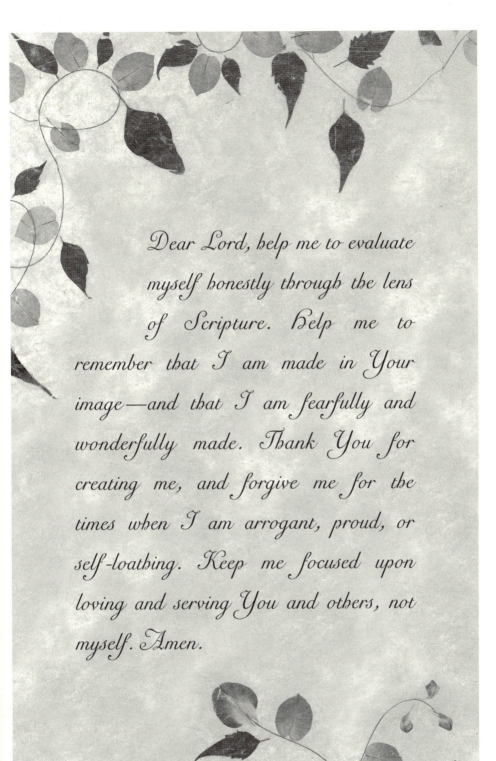

Dear Lord, help me to evaluate myself honestly through the lens of Scripture. Help me to remember that I am made in Your image—and that I am fearfully and wonderfully made. Thank You for creating me, and forgive me for the times when I am arrogant, proud, or self-loathing. Keep me focused upon loving and serving You and others, not myself. Amen.

Chapter 8

I LOVE ME, I LOVE ME NOT

For I say, through the grace given unto me, to every man that is among you, not to think of himself more highly than he ought to think; but to think soberly, according as God hath dealt to every man the measure of faith. (Romans 12:3)

"Did you see the way she flirted around those boys at the church picnic? If she thought more highly of her*self*, then so would everyone else. It's really an issue of low *self*-esteem." (Proverbs 7:21-27)

"Stephanie always seems to be dieting and worrying about her face and hair. She always worries about what others think of her. If only she were more *self*-reliant." (Proverbs 31:30)

"You're always helping other people. Do something for your*self* for a change! You deserve it!" (Luke 14:11)

The three comments above all have one thing in common: they are *self*-centered. Along with many counselors and psychologists, they suppose that a poor self-image—instead of a sinful heart—is the cause of the many woes and mental illnesses of our day. I cannot speak for all families, but in the McDonald household we don't seem to have much trouble with a *lack* of self-esteem. In fact, our trouble seems to be more in getting rid of it. All nine of our children were born with an overabundance of self-preoccupation—most assuredly inherited from their parents.

If we are to view ourselves biblically, it is much more realistic to deal with our depravity swiftly and honestly rather than to agonize over a false sense of our perceived personal *goodness*. Admittedly, trying to locate our "good qualities" is much more fun and far less painful (Proverbs 16:2). It also seems much kinder and gentler to point out the good qualities of others—whether or not those qualities actually exist (Proverbs 27:5-6).

Many young girls today have serious problems (anorexia, bulimia, obesity, promiscuity, drug abuse, alcoholism, and the list goes on). Many individuals are convinced that the answer to the issues young girls face today could simply be solved by a hearty dose of self-esteem. Actually, the search for self-esteem is more than a modern buzz word; it is an age-old pursuit. For years man has thought too highly of himself. Our flesh screams for praise and glory (Genesis 11:4).

The world tells us we are to be proud, daring, and full of self-esteem. God's Word tells us we are to be meek, selfless, and humble (Matthew 5:5, Philippians 2:3, Isaiah 57:15). We would do well to stop petting ourselves like little Agnes in George MacDonald's classic and instead deal honestly with our own wretchedness.

At first Agnes was unaware that the loathsome creature before her eyes was in fact a bizarre physical depiction of how she acted within her own spirit:

When she woke, there was the little girl, heedless, ugly, miserable, staring at her own toes. All at once, the creature began to smile, but with such an odious self-satisfied expression, that Agnes felt ashamed of seeing her. Then she began to pat her own cheeks, to stroke her own body, and examine her finger-ends, nodding her head with satisfaction. Agnes felt that there could not be such another hateful, ape-like creature, and at the same time was perfectly aware she was only doing outside of her what she herself had been doing, as long as she could remember, inside of her.
(*The Wise Woman*, Strahan & Co., 1875)

While writing this chapter, I discussed the subject with my thirteen-year-old daughter, Jessica. Sympathetically she wondered about young people who fall into such a pit of despair that they take their own lives. Even as sheltered as my daughter is, she has been somewhat influenced by the humanistic notion of valuing self-esteem.

"But, Mom," she said, "If they knew how special they were, they wouldn't be overcome by hopelessness. Aren't some people depressed because they just don't think they're any good?"

"Maybe so, but *are* they any good? Are any of us any good?" I asked, raising an eyebrow in her direction.

Knowingly, she smiled, "I see what you mean. It just seems so sad."

Genesis 1:27 tells us we are made in the image of God; therein lies our worth. It *is* very sad that young people don't understand this—but it's because they have rejected the majesty and holiness of the Lord. The answer isn't to give them a false sense of self-importance; the answer is to acknowledge their wickedness, maybe even gently point out their sin, and then joyfully point them to Jesus Christ our Savior, who can cleanse them of that sin. It's their only hope . . . and ours!

And the afflicted people thou wilt save: but thine eyes are upon the haughty, that thou mayest bring them down. For thou art my lamp, O LORD: and the LORD will lighten my darkness. (2 Samuel 22:28-29)

The world wants to find some other way to avoid the *bad* feelings that are the logical result of a sinful life. They want to claim that there is another door through which they can find joy and peace—one that doesn't involve that pesky little annoyance of confessing, repenting, and humbling oneself before a holy God (John 10:1-2, Proverbs 14:12). It is so much easier to believe that our depression is the fault of someone else. "I'm a victim!" is the cry of the people. All the while, the true cause of our misery is our own rebellion against God (Proverbs 28:13).

Ours is an adulterous generation. The reason for the rise in "unwanted" pregnancies (fornication), abortion (murder), homosexuality (sodomy), alcoholism and drug abuse (drunkenness), and suicide (murder and faith in man, rather than God) is *sin*, pure and simple. It's not just the fact that people are sinning; people have been sinning since the fall from grace in the Garden of Eden. Our *response* to the sin is the problem.

Not many years ago, our country held to biblical principles. Sin was treated as sin. Our laws reflected a biblical foundation, and the people—Christians or not—lined up with that thinking. There was a time when it was a shame for a young maiden to even be *alone* with a boy. It was a disgrace to be found pregnant out of wedlock, and abortions were considered. . . *murder*! Homosexuality was so repugnant that it was rarely even whispered about! Now if we turn on the news, abominations are brazenly paraded before our eyes, and we're told that we're judgmental, fanatical, or critical for calling these things sinful.

Such is the way of an adulterous woman; she eateth, and wipeth her mouth, and saith, I have done no wickedness. (Proverbs 30:20)

Sin truly is a burden we can't carry, but to be free of it, we need to stop trying to cover our sins by making excuses for them or blaming others.

If we confess our sins, he is faithful and just to forgive us our sins, and to cleanse us from all unrighteousness. If we say that we have not sinned, we make him a liar, and his word is not in us. (1 John 1:9-10)

Thankfully, God is faithful. His Word tells us that if we confess our sins He will forgive us and cleanse us from *all* unrighteousness, but if we blame others or make excuses for our sin, we make God a liar and we have no hope.

God is a merciful and loving God! He has not left us hopeless and destitute, nor does He regret our existence. He created each of us in the way of His choosing. Did He give you curly hair? That's because it gave Him joy for you to have curly hair. Do you have freckles? It was the Lord who adorned you this way. Are you tall? He didn't create you that way because He likes tall people better than short people, but because it gave Him pleasure for *you* to be tall! He has made each of us for His pleasure and purpose. Not only can we be content with our bodies, but we can humbly rejoice in our own creation!

I will praise thee; for I am fearfully and wonderfully made: marvellous are thy works; and that my soul knoweth right well. My substance was not hid from thee, when I was made in secret, and curiously wrought in the lowest parts of the earth. Thine eyes did see my substance, yet being unperfect; and in thy book all my members were written, which in continuance were fashioned, when as yet there was none of them. How precious also are thy thoughts unto me, O God! how great is the sum of them! If I should count them, they are more in number than the sand: when I awake, I am still with thee. (Psalm 139:14-18)

A healthy recognition of God's love for the people whom He has created and sanctified is one of the first steps to accurately viewing ourselves.

A godly maiden is wise enough to shun the enticement of sugary lies and flattery. She is content in her calling as a pure and wholesome maiden of the Lord, and relies not on her own worth or goodness, but on the grace and mercy of a holy and righteous God. She is armed with the truth of God's Word, she delights in the fearful way in which she is made, and she fully understands that humility and the fear of the Lord are the only riches or honor she needs (Proverbs 22:4).

Share Your Heart

- ᔆ Read Psalm 51:17 and discuss the *sacrifices* that God desires. How does that compare to the message of "self-esteem?"
- ᔆ What do you think is the cause of many of the cases of mental illness today? Read Deuteronomy 28:28, 34 and discuss the curses described.

‰ Read Romans 7:23-25. When Paul says, "O wretched man that I am," do you think he is struggling with self-esteem, or honestly acknowledging his own sin?

‰ Read Proverbs 3:7. When we start thinking we know it all, what typically happens? What does God's Word say about how we should estimate our wisdom?

‰ Read Isaiah 2:12, Psalm 138:6, and 1 Peter 5:5-6. What does God's Word say about His approach to the proud?

‰ Society tells us we need to speak positively about ourselves and celebrates a boastful woman. How does that differ from the words of Proverbs 27:2?

‰ Read Jeremiah 9:23-24. What does Scripture tell us to "glory" in?

‰ Read Matthew 18:1-4, Philippians 2:3, and Mark 9:33-35. What does God's Word say about a desire for attention and praise, or wanting to be first?

‰ Read Luke 15:21. How might the Prodigal Son's reception have been different if he had come home with an arrogant spirit, making excuses, and blaming others?

‰ Read Ephesians 2:8-10. Is there is anything good in us or anything of which we can be proud? For what were we created?

‰ Read Ephesians 3:8 and 1 Timothy 1:15. What should be our attitude toward our own good works?

‰ Read Proverbs 27:5-6. If you are in sin, do you really want someone telling you how *good* you are? Or would you rather someone confront you so that you can be restored to right fellowship with God?

‰ Read Isaiah 57:15. Why is it better to have a contrite and humble spirit?

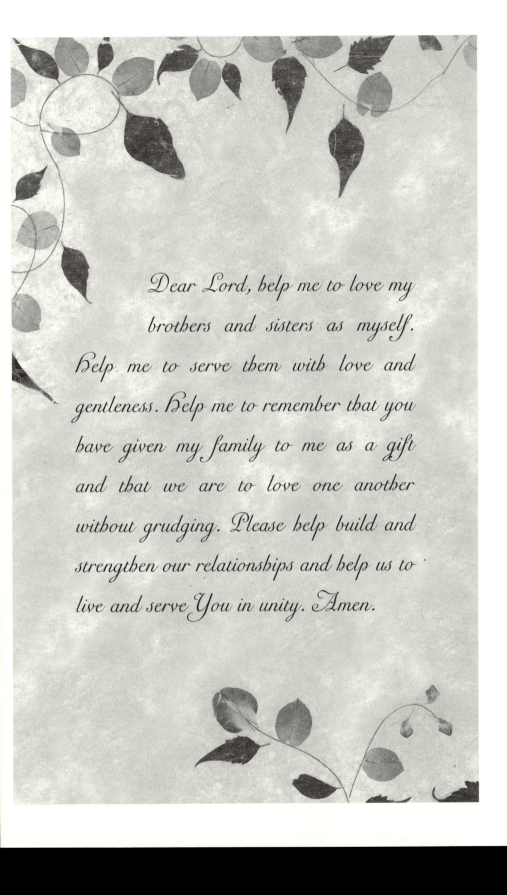

Dear Lord, help me to love my brothers and sisters as myself. Help me to serve them with love and gentleness. Help me to remember that you have given my family to me as a gift and that we are to love one another without grudging. Please help build and strengthen our relationships and help us to live and serve You in unity. Amen.

Chapter 9

DWELLING IN UNITY

Behold, how good and how pleasant it is for brethren to dwell together in unity!
(Psalm 133:1)

Childhood Clapping Song
Say, say, oh, playmate,
Come out and play with me
And bring your dollies three.
Climb up my apple tree.

Slide down my rain barrel
Into my cellar door,
And we'll be jolly friends
Forever more - more - more!

Author Unknown

Despite this song's loyal claims of "forevermore," most people lose touch with their childhood playmates early in their adult years. By the time an average person reaches thirty years of age, she may not be able to recall the names of children she spent long hours with growing up. Sometimes friends are even lost forever immediately following high school graduation. Children grow up, get married, and many times move to different towns,

93

states, or even foreign countries. They begin adult life, leaving behind fond memories of picnics, bike rides, clubhouses, and lemonade stands.

The twenty-something-year-old woman fell into a nostalgic mood while visiting her mother and asked, "Mother, what was the name of that sweet little girl down the street who gave me that pretty red coin purse for my tenth birthday?"

The graying woman seemed amused and looked over her glasses at her daughter. "Honey, I don't remember. That was so long ago, and you had so many different friends over the years."

"But Mom, we played together every day for years! How could you forget?" she asks, straining her own memory.

The mother laughed, "If you yourself can't remember, and *you* are the one who played with her, why do you expect *me* to remember?"

I recall vowing to several different friends in high school that we would *never ever* lose touch. Even if we moved thousands of miles apart, we would talk on the phone every day and visit each other at least once a year. Guess what—we lost touch. We pursued different interests, vocations, and educational choices. When a maiden weds, she dons her husband's name to signify the "leaving and cleaving" of marriage, and new last names can make it nearly impossible to locate old girlfriends.

The truth is that we probably wouldn't have a thing in common anymore anyway. The memories we made together were frivolous, sometimes sinful, and almost always separate from activities with our own families. Incredibly, many of those memories are slowly fading from my remembrance altogether.

The brothers and sisters God gives us in a *family* are different. They are a great blessing and should always be remembered with thankfulness. God places us in families for a particular purpose, and we can be assured it is for our good (Jeremiah 29:11, Romans 8:28). There may be times when siblings don't get along, but the working out of those relationships is what helps us to grow. God uses conflict to stretch us.

One of my favorite board games is *Taboo*™. I love to play it with the children as a family. Even more, I love to play it when another family is visiting. I especially like to watch my children team up against another sibling group because it is such a wonderful reminder of the way God is working unity in our family.

You see, the reason sibling-groups work so well in this game is because to successfully help your teammates guess the correct answer, you must really *know* each other. The most successful teams have made the same memories together, have shared the same jokes, know the same songs, and recognize each other's expressions. Sometimes while playing, one of the children will need to give only a one-word clue or even a look and the other child immediately guesses the answer correctly. The other group is usually astonished—unless it's another sibling team that is just as close-knit. I love the fact that my children know each other so well! I pray that it is always so, and I pray that it is so in your family. If it's not, I have good news: it can be!

One day all of my children will most likely marry and begin their own households, but the family bond that we have is not one that will fade away from memory. My oldest daughter won't be sitting beside me one day trying to recall the name of one of her siblings. That is the way of families. Though children grow up, their newly-formed families are still intricately connected and we hope still very actively involved with one another.

My husband and I hope to be a huge part of our grandchildren's and great-grandchildren's lives. I want to be with my daughters and daughters-in-law when their children are born—helping them after childbirth and assisting them in their duties. My husband looks forward to the day when he can be a grandpa and build castles with his grandbabies while sharing the truths of God's *heavenly* kingdom with them. A family should have a generational vision—and the way a maiden relates to her parents and siblings is an important part of that vision.

The fact is, most families today are in trouble. Part of the problem results from rarely being around one another. Group schooling, sports clubs, and church youth groups have all contributed to the fragmentation and breakdown of the family. Simple activities such as eating dinner at the table together are a thing of the past in most families. They all seem to have their own busy and very legitimate-sounding activities that keep them apart from those whom God has given them.

Why do you think children on sports teams and in youth groups become close friends? They are typically working together toward some sort of goal—winning a game or washing cars to save up for a special event. The same thing happens on mission trips and in dorms. The people we eat, work, sweat, and travail with are those with whom we become close. Why isn't this happening in more *families* instead of with perfect strangers?

One thing you can do as a young maiden to develop strong bonds with your siblings is to make yourself available to them. Be willing to listen when your little brother wants to tell you about his rock for the fourth time. Color with your little sister—even if she wants to use only the purple crayon for the entire picture; enjoy her and look for the beauty in what she has created. Ask the sister you have been having difficulties getting along with to go for a walk—just the two of you. Spend time cooking, sharing chores, playing games, folding laundry, and singing or playing instruments together. All these activities create memories and build relationships.

Remember to create a habit of speaking kindly to your siblings. Even if you have been spoken to harshly, you can respond in gentleness (Proverbs 15:1). If you have been treated cruelly, remember Paul's call to the elect of God (Colossians 3:12-13). You may find that you have won a brother or diffused an argument before it even starts. You will also have benefited by establishing a wonderful habit of understanding and mercy that will carry over into your marriage and into motherhood. Remember also to forgive others just as you wish to be forgiven. (Mark 11:25-26)

Swiftly asking for forgiveness when you have offended a brother or sister (purposely or not) is a sure way to keep peace in the house. Remember that many disagreements are a result of poor communication. Sometimes finding a quiet spot to pray and write a letter to your sibling is a wonderful way to mend bridges and restore a damaged relationship. This way you have time to pray and carefully choose your words.

One day when you are grown and find yourself in the midst of a trial or heartbreak, it won't be the girl who gave you the coin purse on your tenth birthday that you call. It will be your brother, your sister, your *family* that you will want by your side. When you discover for yourself the truth of Genesis 3:19, and the day arrives when your parents go to be with the Lord, who is going to share your loss more than your brothers and sisters?

Remember that your family is given as a gift. Encourage and love one another. Cherish the time you have been given and know that the memories you make now will be with you always. In twenty years it won't matter much whether or not your sister left her clothes on the floor after you reminded her three times to pick them up, but it will matter a great deal whether or not you held her hand when she was scared. Love one another, remembering that you are building a heritage of faithfulness.

I suggest we make a priority of making our brothers and sisters our best friends. We can begin by changing our tune:

Say, Say, Oh, Sister
Say, say, oh, sister,
Come here and sit with me
And bring our brothers three.
We'll sing in harmony.

Let's play a board game
Or walk the sandy shore
And we'll be jolly friends
Forever more - more - more!

Share Your Heart

- What are some ways you can include your siblings in your life? When one of your siblings is completing a chore, could you voluntarily jump in to help?

- Purpose to say something encouraging to your siblings each day. Either notice something they have done well or something they have done that is helpful, or remind them of a sweet memory from the past.

- Try to remember to use physical gestures of affection. Touch your sister's hand, pat your brother's shoulder, or kiss your little brother or sister at bedtime to remind them that you love them.

- Write letters or notes of encouragement to your siblings. Buy a small package of sticky notes and write verses of Scripture or edifying comments that express your love for your siblings. Post the notes on their bathroom mirror where they will find them in the morning while brushing their teeth.

- Prepare a picnic lunch and send your sibling a "formal" invitation to join you.

- Plan a "sister tea party" or a "brother tea party" (our sons like masculine English tea parties!) and invite the appropriate siblings. Come prepared with edifying words and good discussion topics. With either brothers or sisters, this could be a real memory maker!

- Write a poem for a brother or sister.

- Write a fictional story and include all your siblings as characters. (Make sure they are not the villains of your story!)

  As you bring these same loving habits and gestures of affection into your future marriage, it will be a great blessing to your husband as well.

Dear Lord, place a guard before my lips. Help me to speak words that edify others and glorify You. Keep me from words that harm and destroy. Place in my mouth the law of kindness, and grant me wisdom that I might praise Your name forever. Amen.

Chapter 10

TAMING THE TONGUE

Let no corrupt communication proceed out of your mouth, but that which is good to the use of edifying, that it may minister grace unto the hearers. And grieve not the holy Spirit of God, whereby ye are sealed unto the day of redemption. Let all bitterness, and wrath, and anger, and clamour, and evil speaking, be put away from you, with all malice: And be ye kind one to another, tenderhearted, forgiving one another, even as God for Christ's sake hath forgiven you. (Ephesians 4:29-32)

The crisp Virginia air spurred the extra energy in Lydia's step this chilly fall morning. The aroma of burning logs and falling leaves stirred warm memories of family and good times. Chimneys puffed with smoke throughout the neighborhood, hinting at the cozy hearth scenes within each neat house. Contentedly she pulled her shawl around her head to block the wind.

Lydia thought about the warm spiced pumpkin muffins awaiting her when she arrived home, and she increased her pace. Cheerfully heading toward her own winding street, Lydia wondered if ever there had ever been a more glorious morning . . . but before she could finish her thought, she came across a group of children gathered in the school yard on the corner.

Playground Daggers

She slowed her pace to observe the curious scene. At first she thought they were playing, until a distinctly cutting tone echoed across the old colonial path. "Where did you get that *nice* coat?" taunted a fat, freckle-faced boy.

"Yeah, it's so . . . pre-e-e-tty," giggled a few girls.

A frail child in a faded red coat stood fearfully facing her persecutors. "My Aunt Ellie gave it to me—it's warm. . . I have to go home now," she sniffed. Her large green eyes welled with tears as she attempted to walk past the bully who was casually blocking her way.

"What's wrong with your hood—did a dog chew off all the fur?" he teased. "Look!" He pointed at the helpless girl. "It's Little Red Riding Waif!"

The combined laughter from the crowd of unruly children seemed to merge into one hideous voice. "Little Red Riding Waif!" they joined in mercilessly. "Are you going to see your grandmother?" More laughter ensued. "Watch out for the wolf, Little Red Riding Waif!" they chanted.

When it became clear that the boy was having too much fun to let her pass, the poor girl put her hands on her hips and bravely looked the bully in the eye. "Leave me alone! Sticks and stone will break my bones, but words will never hurt me," she quipped.

The boy sneered, "Well, maybe we need to go get some sticks and stones." Slowly he turned to his friends as if to draw more venom from the crowd. They roared with cruel laughter.

Lydia could not stand it any longer. Furiously, she flew into the school yard and, with tears of righteous indignation, stood between the little girl and the bully. At the sight of a near-adult (she was sixteen and very tall), all the children scattered—all but the weeping little girl, who crumpled to the ground in sorrow.

Lydia covered the sobbing child with her shawl and spoke kindly to her. She shared with her the story of Joseph from the Bible. She described his jealous brothers and their plot to kill him. The little girl's eyes grew wide as she learned of Joseph's special coat of many colors and how God was eventually glorified through Joseph's trials. The girl listened intently as Lydia told her all about God and his mysterious ways of working things out for the ultimate good of His people—even when things seem so painful and confusing.

She openeth her mouth with wisdom; and in her tongue is the law of kindness.
(Proverbs 31:26)

When the child seemed sufficiently comforted, Lydia walked her home and promised to check on her later in the day. Lydia had made a friend.

Upon arriving home, Lydia shared with her mother the incident in the school yard. The wise woman listened carefully as her daughter recounted the cruel morning scene. Deeply inhaling the scent of cinnamon and cloves, Lydia covered the basket of steaming muffins and decided to take some to her new friend later.

Who Me?

"Mother, I can't imagine that anyone could be so mean. It was as if they enjoyed causing that sweet girl pain," Lydia vented.

"You're right, honey, it was a mean thing to do. I guess some things never change," she sighed. "I find it interesting that children still use the same pathetic nursery rhyme about sticks and stones and broken bones. At least broken bones can heal; cutting words are like a poisonous dagger, and sometimes careless or cruel words leave scars that stay with us always. Without God's grace, some people never fully recover from the harsh words of others. God can and does heal our hurts, but sometimes painful memories still linger and resurface during low times. Words can destroy relationships, harm marriages, damage children, and split churches. God warns us about the power of the tongue.

"When we imagine sins of the tongue, we tend to think of gossip, cursing, or lying. What you witnessed today was an example of purposeful verbal nastiness. But sometimes our careless words are just as injurious within our own families— maybe more so. Sometimes a careless remark to a sibling about some physical feature or a hasty joke about a peculiar habit or personal quirk is hurtful.

"Do you remember last week when you and your sister Jennifer were arguing? She had pointed out your unmade bed and lack of diligence in keeping things as neat as you probably should. When your feelings were hurt by her drawn-out rebuke, you said some rather unkind things about her cooking skills. God's Word tells us:

> *"A soft answer turneth away wrath: but grievous words stir up anger. The tongue of the wise useth knowledge aright: but the mouth of fools poureth out foolishness."* (Proverbs 15:1-2)

Lydia winced as she remembered the sarcastic way she had suggested that Jennifer would probably never make much more than boxed macaroni and cheese and instant pudding for her future husband and children. She had taunted Jennifer with a few more comments about her most recent cooking failures before she had gone to bed angry that night. How had she developed such a caustic tongue?

> *Even so the tongue is a little member, and boasteth great things. Behold, how great a matter a little fire kindleth! And the tongue is a fire, a world of iniquity: so is the tongue among our members, that it defileth the whole body, and setteth on fire the course of nature; and it is set on fire of hell.* (James 3:5-6)

"Yesterday after dinner," Lydia's mother softly reminded her, "I noticed Jennifer fighting back tears when one of the boys made a slight comment about the gravy being lumpy. I know she wouldn't have thought much of what an eight-year-old thought of the gravy, especially after his third helping, had she not already been wounded by your words about her cooking."

With a lump in her throat, Lydia looked at the floor. "Oh Mom, do you really think she believes I don't consider her a good cook? I was just angry because of what she had said about . . . oh . . . I was trying to *hurt* her. Mother, do you believe I'm as bad as those cruel children in the school yard?" Lydia lamented.

Lydia's mother tenderly continued, "I believe that my girls love each other very much but haven't yet learned to harness the fiery power of the tongue. As beautifully gentle, helpful, and dutiful as you are, if you never learn to tame your tongue, the Bible says you are deceived and that your good works are in vain. James reminds us that:

If any man among you seem to be religious, and bridleth not his tongue, but deceiveth his own heart, this man's religion is vain. (James 1:26)

"God's Word gives us many examples of what sort of sins pour forth from the tongue: lying, gossiping, backbiting, coarse jesting, complaining, murmuring, tattling, slandering, flattering—the list goes on. Women in particular seem to have a difficult time using the tongue for God's glory."

The young maiden's mother continued, "You may use your bridled tongue as a great blessing to those you nurture and serve—a blessing of mercy, love, comfort, and compassion—the way you did with the child in the school yard. But if you are not careful, you may easily slip into gossip, idle talk, complaining, or nagging. You may become critical of others or even develop a contentious spirit (Proverbs 25:24).

"The next time you are tempted to wield your tongue in a way that may hurt someone else, I want you to remember the grief you felt for that little girl today, and count the cost. Check your heart for deception—for bitterness, jealousy, or anger. There may be times when you are forced to speak the truth to someone in love—truth that may in fact hurt them, but make sure it's for their ultimate good, and make sure it is truly done in love" (Ephesians 4:15).

Lydia realized she needed to ask Jennifer for forgiveness. She couldn't wait to make things right between them again. She purposed right then to pray daily and ask God to set a watch over her mouth. She thanked God for allowing her to walk past the school yard at just the right time. Not only was she able to defend someone in need, but God actually used this little girl to teach her a great truth.

Let no corrupt communication proceed out of your mouth, but that which is good to the use of edifying, that it may minister grace unto the hearers. And grieve not the holy Spirit of God, whereby ye are sealed unto the day of redemption. Let all bitterness, and wrath, and anger, and clamour, and evil speaking, be put away from you, with all malice: And be ye kind one to another, tenderhearted, forgiving one another, even as God for Christ's sake hath forgiven you. (Ephesians 4:29-32)

She bit into one of the moist muffins. The cinnamon toasty top complemented the warm buttery center and reminded her of why she loved this time of year. At that moment, Jennifer walked into the room. In her eagerness to make things right with her sister she forgot that her mouth was full. She garbled, "Jen, would you like to come awong wif me?" She laughed, swallowed, and wiped her mouth. "I'm going to deliver these muffins Mama made to a family I met today." Lydia took another hungry bite.

Jennifer looked at her curiously. "Do you *like* those muffins?" She asked teasingly.

Realizing her meaning, Lydia stopped chewing. "Did *you* make these muffins?" Jennifer smiled.

"These are even better than what Mama made last year! They're wonderful! Oh, Jennifer, I am so sorry for what I said about your cooking. You know it's not true!"

Lydia poured her heart out to her sister, asking for her forgiveness and confessing her own hurts. As the girls restored their friendship, Lydia asked Jennifer if she would like to join her for a walk to deliver a basket of incredibly luscious pumpkin muffins to a very special little girl.

Set a watch, O Lord, before my mouth; keep the door of my lips. (Psalm 141:3)

Share Your Heart

- ✍ Read James 3:8-10. Think of a time when you were hurt by the careless words of another. Did those words feel like poison? If this person had slapped you, would you still remember the pain of that slap in as much detail as you do today? Discuss how much more hurtful words are than physical pain.

❧ Read Matthew 12:36-37. Can you remember a time when you hurt someone else by using hasty words, careless joking, or teasing? Have you ever accused others of being overly sensitive due to your own harsh words?

❧ Read James 1:26. Discuss what a bridle is and how it works. Can a horse put a bridle on himself? Who is strong enough to steer and control the tongue?

❧ Read Colossians 3:8. An angry spirit, bitterness, or jealousy makes it difficult to control the tongue. Scripture teaches us in Matthew 15:19-20 that what defiles a man is not what can be washed from his hands, but what comes from his heart (which can only be washed by the Lord). He tells us that what comes out of a man's heart (evil motives, wicked thoughts, hatred, blasphemies) is what pollutes us. Purpose to pray each day and ask God to show you your sin so that you may confess it and turn to Him in hope. Ask Him to bridle your tongue and set a guard over your mouth.

❧ Read Proverbs 25:28. Discuss how self-control can help us to avoid sinning.

❧ According to 1 Peter 3:1-2, how can a woman's tongue affect her marriage?

❧ Read James 3:8. Why do you think the tongue is described as being full of deadly poison?

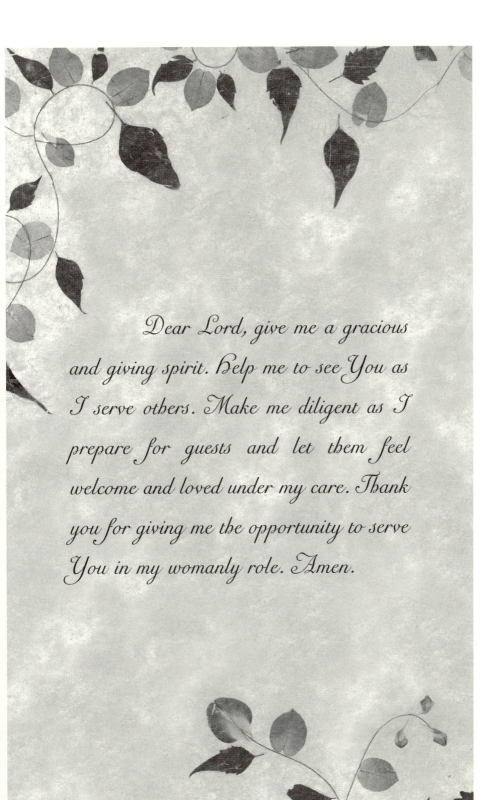

Dear Lord, give me a gracious and giving spirit. Help me to see You as I serve others. Make me diligent as I prepare for guests and let them feel welcome and loved under my care. Thank you for giving me the opportunity to serve You in my womanly role. Amen.

Chapter 11

THE CHEERFUL VOICE OF HOSPITALITY

Use hospitality one to another without grudging. (1 Peter 4:9)

Travel-weary and hungry, our family arrived in town just before dark. My six-year-old brother Thomas had fallen asleep upright in the backseat, hugging his bear. Papa peered at each house number trying to find the address for our friends, the Millers.

"There it is," Mama said, "5526, the house with the geraniums by the mailbox!"

Mama carried the baby while I, being the oldest boy, helped Papa with the luggage. Thomas cuddled closer to his bear in the backseat. "Are we there yet?" he purred sleepily.

The scent of cinnamon and cloves drifted out to greet us as we stood on the porch. Suddenly the door flew open, and we were ushered in by a happy crowd of curly-blonde Miller children.

"Here, let me carry that for you," they all seemed to say at once. The oldest daughter added, "Can I get you something to drink?"

The eight-year-old Miller son proudly chirped, "Mama said you're sleepin' in my room, so I cleaned it extra special!"

Mr. and Mrs. Miller met us in the doorway grinning. Mama hugged Mrs. Miller and whispered her thankfulness for good friends and warm welcomes, and

Papa and Mr. Miller shook hands. Thomas smiled as the youngest Miller girl giggled and offered him a toy.

The Millers' house was warm and cozy, and without a word, we somehow knew we were welcome. Fresh fruit, cheese, and warm homemade bread were waiting for us in the parlor. The oldest Miller daughter served us herbal tea in little teacups that made me think of Benjamin Bunny and his kind old mother.

The beautiful violin music that drifted through the house enhanced the conversation rather than suppressed it.

Mrs. Miller and her daughters served our family with joy and ease. It seemed so natural—as if they were doing what they were created to do.

I observed how Mr. Miller pulled back Mrs. Miller's chair before she sat, and I noticed a lump in my own throat as he prayed over our meal at dinner with such passion and genuine gratefulness to his God.

Later that evening we found our rooms carefully prepared with fresh herbs and flowers by the bedside, soft sheets, and warm snuggly quilts on the beds. Floral-scented linen baskets complete with little shampoos, soaps, and a Bible sat on an old trunk in the corner.

As I slept under the warm comforter that night, the lavender potpourri stirred pleasant thoughts of our friends the Millers. I wondered what it was that made me feel so warm and good when we were here.

The Millers were Christians, but I had met Christians before—the man screaming on television and asking for money was a Christian. And the lady who lives next door to us must be a Christian because she has one of those fish symbols on her car—and she handed me a gospel tract once—but she must not like being a Christian much because she never smiles. Mr. and Mrs. Miller seem to smile all the time. But Papa says the Millers are a different kind of Christian.

Papa says being around the Millers makes him consider his ways. Tonight I saw him sitting in the corner thumbing through the Bible the Millers left in our guest towel basket. I wonder if being at the Millers' house makes Papa feel sad inside instead of warm and good like it does me, because just as I was drifting off to sleep, I saw Mama kneeling beside Papa and I could have sworn I heard him weeping.

———————◆———————

There are few ways in which a Christian family can communicate the love and goodness of Christ better than by practicing hospitality. Instead of putting our individual activities and self-centered pleasures above serving others, we can experience the joy of honoring and blessing other families or individuals with various forms of hospitality and service.

By showing hospitality to others, specifically *unbelievers*, a family exemplifies the Gospel in a living way. By revealing what a godly Christian marriage looks like, your parents demonstrate the wonder of Christ and His Bride. By honoring your father and serving in your role as a maidenly daughter in your home, you display the appeal and loveliness of contented femininity. Showing that a Christian family can work together in love to bless and honor someone else beautifully communicates the scriptural directive of putting others before ourselves.

Living out our Christianity in this fashion enables us to develop relationships and credibility with our guests. We may even be asked how in the world our family can function as it does. As God goes before us in this way, we are then ready to share the answer.

Since our righteousness is not due to our own personal human enlightenment, mere coincidence, or any unique spark of goodness we possess on our own, we have the opportunity to testify of the One to whom all glory and honor *are* due. We can tell of our gratefulness for the inestimable grace and love of our Savior and the power that He has to cleanse us of our sins and transform our families. Compare this ancient method of communicating the Gospel to the modern practice of passing out Christian tracts or street witnessing, and you may decide that you have found a quite natural ministry for your family—one where the whole family can be involved. Additionally, because most young ladies of the world are not consistently preparing for their future roles as wives and mothers (maybe they are chasing selfish ambitions or pursuing careers) the Christian maiden at home has a particularly unique opportunity to communicate Christ by her purity, loveliness, and willingness to serve.

Hospitality does not necessarily mean fine china teacups and soft downy quilts. It may simply mean a glass of cold water on a hot summer's day or a warm cup of cocoa for the mailman on a blustery afternoon. Either way, it shows a spirit of service and love, and it allows us to function biblically in our everyday lives, all within the roles in which He has placed us.

Imagine how the simple example of a godly, loving family working together and joyfully serving others at hearth and home speak honestly of the transforming power and loving nature of God. Consider how communicating the Gospel in a living way, within the biblical roles of a real family, can be an effective means of exemplifying the grace of God and causing others to "consider their ways." When we seek God's wisdom and strength in living our lives and glorifying Him with all we have and do, we communicate Him and His Truth to the world.

Share Your Heart

- Consider the young man's statement: "Mrs. Miller and her daughters served our family with joy and ease. It seemed so natural—as if they were doing what they were created to do." What do you think he meant? How could this ministry opportunity have been lost if Mrs. Miller had to serve alone because her daughters were at camp, part-time jobs, a youth group function, or "out" with friends?

- Discuss how a spirit of "service" and "hospitality" go hand in hand. Do you enjoy serving others? Discuss and plan possible opportunities you have to serve others—especially in ways that complement your femininity. (Chopping firewood for a neighbor may not be a good choice, but serving a meal to a family with a new baby or nursing a sick relative or elderly person would be a great one!)

- Look up the following Scriptures:
  - Romans 12:13
  - Galatians 6:10
  - 1 Timothy 3:2
  - Titus 1:8
  - 1 Peter 4:9
  - Hebrews 13:2
  - Matthew 20:26-28
  - 1 Corinthians 10:24
  - Philippians 2:3-8

- Now look up the words "hospitality" and "service" in the dictionary and discuss God's purpose for both.

- By actively embracing your biblical role in the home, how can you "communicate the gospel" without necessarily *preaching* to anyone?

- Read Luke 14:12-14. Discuss how practicing hospitality or serving those who cannot repay us with a reciprocal invitation or aid can glorify God the most. What are some practical ways to serve this way— inside and outside the home?

- Read Luke 10:38-42. Discuss how present busyness and the lack of prayer and fellowship with God might hinder a peaceful and God-glorifying fellowship with friends later.

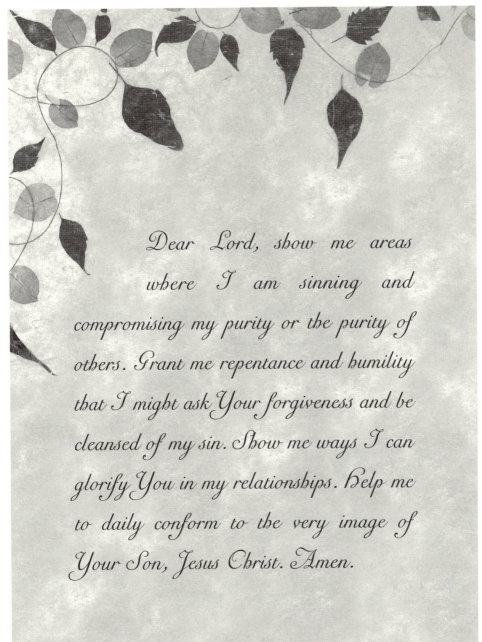

Dear Lord, show me areas where I am sinning and compromising my purity or the purity of others. Grant me repentance and humility that I might ask Your forgiveness and be cleansed of my sin. Show me ways I can glorify You in my relationships. Help me to daily conform to the very image of Your Son, Jesus Christ. Amen.

Chapter 12

TINKLING FEET

Moreover the LORD saith, Because the daughters of Zion are haughty, and walk with stretched forth necks and wanton eyes, walking and mincing as they go, and making a tinkling with their feet: Therefore the Lord will smite with a scab the crown of the head of the daughters of Zion, and the LORD will discover their secret parts.
(Isaiah 3:16-17)

In the mid-eighties the pop singer Madonna was all the rage. Her hit song "Like a Virgin" caused star-struck teenyboppers across the nation to throw caution to the wind and brazenly imitate the rhinestone starlet. It seemed everyone wanted to dress like Madonna—which was not "like a virgin" at all.

Apparently the more tinkling bracelets, gaudy crosses, dangly earrings, and layered necklaces one wore, the more attractive one became. Combinations of lace, black leather, gaudy makeup, and pink *everything* were swirled together to evoke a spirit of unruly sensuality—with a hint of make-believe innocence.

Another hit song by Madonna was "Material Girl," and this time the name fit the lyrics. These lyrics at least spoke honestly of her desire for things of the flesh—material things—and how she only paid attention to the boy with the "cold hard cash."

Modern Mandy

Today we have a new kind of "material girl," and she does not look "like a virgin" either. Even if she is not after the boy with the "cold hard cash," she is just as self-centered.

Modern Mandy, today's average young woman, has pierced body parts which demonstrate her strange fascination with bondage, death, and destruction. The unnatural shade of her lipstick and nail polish reveal Mandy's fondness for the unconventional. She loves jewelry with strange symbols and rebellious slogans. Ironically, sometimes the phrases include words like "peace" or "free" this or that. Funny—this material girl doesn't seem peaceful, and the only thing she appears truly *free* of is joy.

Lately, Modern Mandy has been dead set on showing us her navel. Short skirts and low-cut tops are her attire of choice, and she cares little whether or not her exhibitionist-style clothing upsets her parents or anyone else.

Since Mandy's hair usually hangs in her face, it may be difficult to notice that she rarely smiles—smirking doesn't count. But, regardless of her hairstyle, her general look of disrespect, defiance, and boredom is unmistakable and the rebellion in her heart is not just evidenced in her outward appearance. Her lazy, self-centered attitude is apparent any time her mother asks her to help with household tasks: she rolls her eyes and her neck stiffens. Even simple chores like cleaning her own room or doing her school work throw Mandy into fits of indignation.

Sadly, Mandy considers her younger siblings a "nuisance." Her younger sister is always "snooping in her stuff," and her little brother constantly makes the "most annoying noises." None of Mandy's friends get along with their brothers and sisters. She believes it is *normal* to treat siblings like infuriating bothers. Besides, she would much rather watch television, go to the mall, or be around her friends than her family. They have been growing more and more distant anyway.

Mandy has numerous male buddies who are all just *friends*. One boy seems to like her more than the others. She finds herself strangely amused when she catches him staring at her when she wears certain clothes. She has even made a game of catching his eye and purposely making him blush. Of course he's just a friend to her—if he can't control himself, that's *his* problem (Proverbs 6:25-26).

What stands out even more than Mandy's gloomy makeup and distasteful appearance is her lack of dignity. She may momentarily enjoy the negative attention she gets, but it doesn't satisfy her. Instead it leaves her with an empty gnawing in the pit of her stomach. She yearns to feel clean and truly loved.

Sure, she has a bit of a bad attitude, but what did we expect—she's not a Christian. What's the big deal anyway? After all, a girl needs to be comfortable. Shouldn't we do what we *feel* is right? Doesn't God just look at the inside? Isn't it natural for a girl to want to be independent of her family and to be irritated by annoying siblings? Isn't that all part of growing up? Isn't that *normal*?

An Impure Facade

The problem is that we have mimicked the world for so long—copying their fashions, borrowing their educational and social philosophies, conforming to their dating format, and adopting their dialect—that we do not even realize we have lost our Christian identity. We've been wearing the costume and speaking the language of the world for so long that we don't even recognize ourselves anymore.

> *Dearly beloved, I beseech you as strangers and pilgrims, abstain from fleshly lusts, which war against the soul; Having your conversation honest among the Gentiles: that, whereas they speak against you as evildoers, they may by your good works, which they shall behold, glorify God in the day of visitation.* (1 Peter 2:11-12)

If we Christian women do not show Mandy what biblical beauty, femininity, and modesty look like, how is she to know? But then again, how are *we* to know? Who is going to show *us*? We ourselves have forgotten.

If we visit most any church youth group, we will see young ladies who speak, walk, dress, talk, and flirt exactly like the daughters of the heathen. This has happened as a result of our conformity to the world—and the Church doesn't even realize it. Instead, Christians must be *conformed* to the image of Christ, and it is imperative that our uniqueness be evident to the world (Romans 8:29).

As obedient children, not fashioning yourselves according to the former lusts in your ignorance: But as he which hath called you is holy, so be ye holy in all manner of conversation; Because it is written, Be ye holy; for I am holy. (1 Peter 1:14-16)

It has been said that imitation is the highest form of flattery. We tend to imitate those of whom we think highly—those we decide we would like to be like. So if we imitate the world, what are we communicating?

Though Mandy is a fictitious character who also happens to be an unbeliever, what can we learn from her? How can you make sure that you resemble a Maiden of Virtue rather than a Modern Mandy?

Instead of mirroring Mandy's behavior or appearance, show her (and her parents) that there is something better—something wholesome, pure, and lovely. You are the very one who may demonstrate to the Madonnas and Mandys of the world what virginity is all about. Prove to the world that virginity is more than saving one single biological act for marriage: it's a way of thinking, a way of living, a general state of being. Instead of dressing like a dime-store floozy and singing about feeling *like* a virgin, you can show Modern Mandy the beauty and joy of actually *being* one—physically as well as spiritually.

Your affection for your siblings will demonstrate a gracious spirit and a unique maturity that is seldom seen in the world. As a Christian maiden, the mercy you have received from your Lord should carry over to the way you treat your brothers and sisters, expressing a spirit of meekness, humility, and love—even when they make annoying noises or snoop in your stuff.

Whose adorning let it not be that outward adorning of plaiting the hair, and of wearing of gold, or of putting on of apparel; But let it be the hidden man of the heart, in that which is not corruptible, even the ornament of a meek and quiet spir-

it, which is in the sight of God of great price. For after this manner in the old time
the holy women also, who trusted in God, adorned themselves, being in subjection
unto their own husband. (1 Peter 3:3-5)

In this passage the Apostle Peter was warning us of investing all of our efforts in trying to beautify our bodies to the detriment of our souls.

Have you ever met a woman who was very beautiful until you got to know her? Maybe her vanity or her mean spirit caused you to wonder what you thought was so beautiful to begin with. This is what is meant by the "hidden man of the heart." Our adornment is evident in our demeanor, speech, and behavior. 1 Timothy 2:10 tells us that a woman professing godliness will adorn herself in good works. Which is truly more beautiful: A pretty face with a mean spirit, or a plain face crowned with a meek and gentle spirit, busy with good works?

As a jewel of gold in a swine's snout, so is a fair woman which is without discretion.
(Proverbs 11:22)

There are many places in Scripture that allow for and even encourage beautiful adornment in moderation. Ezekiel 16:11-15 tells us of God's allowance for outward ornamentation, while giving a stern warning against the pride that can accompany feminine beauty. It's also a reminder of *who* makes us beautiful:

I decked thee also with ornaments, and I put bracelets upon thy hands, and a chain
on thy neck. And I put a jewel on thy forehead, and earrings in thine ears, and a
beautiful crown upon thine head...And thy renown went forth among the heathen
for thy beauty: for it was perfect through my comeliness, which I had put upon thee,"
saith the Lord GOD. But thou didst trust in thine own beauty, and playedst the har-
lot because of thy renown, and pouredst out thy fornications on every one that

passed by; his it was.

Scripture does not tell us that pretty clothes are sinful. Being prideful, covetous, or using our beauty for wickedness is sinful. There are many examples where fine clothes are positively exemplified in Scripture. It's important to let the beauty of the Lord show through in our outward appearance as well as our inward spirit—because actually, what we choose to wear will be a reflection of what's on the inside anyway.

> *She maketh herself coverings of tapestry; her clothing is silk and purple.*
> (Proverbs 31:22)

> *I clothed thee also with broidered work, and shod thee with badgers' skin, and I girded thee about with fine linen, and I covered thee with silk.* (Ezekiel 16:10)

> *The king's daughter is all glorious within: her clothing is of wrought gold.*
> (Psalm 45:13)

A young maiden should ask, "Who am I wearing this for and why?" All to the glory of God! Let 1 Corinthians 10:31-33 help direct your choices in outward adornment.

As a pure and delicate flower emerges from the earth, unfolds, and reaches toward the sun for nourishment and light, you too will rise up from the ashes of ruin and decay that is our modern culture, stretching and growing toward the cleansing power and goodness of our Savior. Then, in awed silence, a lost and dying world will turn and behold a spotless bride and know the beauty and radiance of Christ.

Share Your Heart

Read Proverbs 6:23-26 and discuss the following questions:

❧ What do you think Scripture means when it warns a man not to allow a whorish woman to "take" him "with her eyelids?"

❧ What are some other ways the scene in Proverbs 6:25 is played out today?

❧ What was the "attire of an harlot" that Scripture refers to? Can someone dress like a harlot and still be covered appropriately from head to toe?

❧ What does Proverbs 6:24 say about a woman who uses her tongue to flatter a young man? What do you think her true motives are? Why do you think a foolish young man would fall for her dishonest tactics?

❧ Read Romans 14:13-21. If a maiden dresses immodestly, how could it harm a young man? How could it hurt his future or current wife? Would her carelessness show a loving attitude towards her neighbor?

❧ How could dressing in a certain manner be considered selfish?

❧ Read Isaiah 3:16 and discuss the following questions:

❧ What are "tinkling feet"?

❧ What does it mean to "mince as they go"?

❧ What does it mean to have an "outstretched neck"?

❧ Read 1 Peter 3:3-5. What incorruptible adornment is so precious to the Lord in this verse?

❧ Read Proverbs 12:15 and discuss how this type of fool is alive and well today.

❧ Prayerfully read and discuss Titus 2:5.

❧ If we publicly expose our bodies or wear clothing that accentuates our private areas, are we being discreet?

❧ How could not being discreet or chaste blaspheme the Word of God?

❧ What responsibility, if any, does a Christian maiden have to help prevent lust in her brother?

❧ If we know that flaunting our bodies causes boys or men to be stirred to lust and we do it anyway, are we being modest, or are we trying to draw attention to ourselves so that we may feel more important or desirable?

❧ Which terms do you feel would accurately describe Mandy or her lifestyle? Which describe a godly fair maiden? Discuss the reasons for your choices:

trustworthy	loose	chick	silly
innocent	bold	babe	demure
kind	shamefaced	lovely	brave
meek	productive	cool	frugal
beautiful	compassionate	gentle	selfish
shocking	popular	honorable	whiner
virtuous	grumbler	vain	loyal
praiseworthy	excellent	chaste	lazy
maiden	exciting	virgin	joyful
girl	pure	quiet	sloppy
tough	strange	wise	modest
forward	flirtatious	resourceful	merciful
intelligent	idle	strong	flatterer
lady			

❧ Ask the Lord to show you and your mother how many of the preceding characteristics describe *you*.

❧ Do you see any areas in which you need to change? Ask your mother to pray with you and help you work on these areas.

❧ Mother, share with your maiden(s) areas where you struggled when you were younger. How did God change your heart?

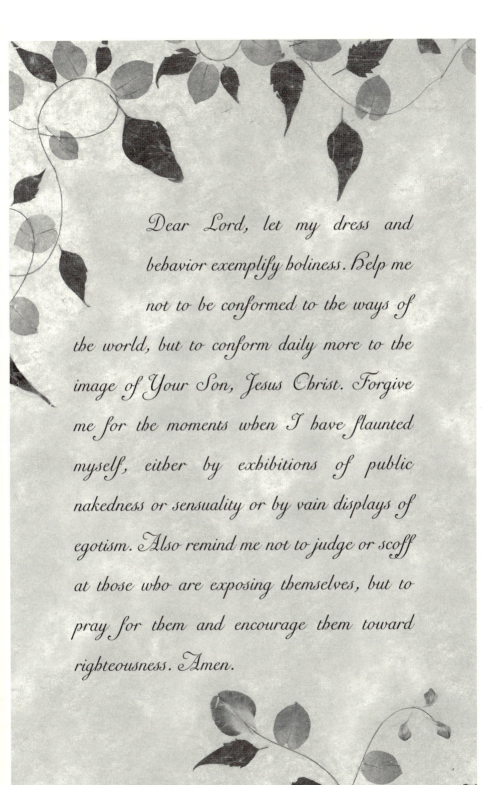

Dear Lord, let my dress and behavior exemplify holiness. Help me not to be conformed to the ways of the world, but to conform daily more to the image of Your Son, Jesus Christ. Forgive me for the moments when I have flaunted myself, either by exhibitions of public nakedness or sensuality or by vain displays of egotism. Also remind me not to judge or scoff at those who are exposing themselves, but to pray for them and encourage them toward righteousness. Amen.

Chapter 13

COLORFUL FLAMINGOS

Take the millstones, and grind meal: uncover thy locks, make bare the leg, uncover the thigh, pass over the rivers. Thy nakedness shall be uncovered, yea, thy shame shall be seen: I will take vengeance, and I will not meet thee as a man. (Isaiah 47:2-3)

ave you ever seen a flamingo? You know—the bird with the long legs and bright pink, ostentatious feathers? Do these pink show-stoppers remind you of anyone?

While accompanying my husband on a business trip recently, my daughter Melissa and I learned something new about flamingos: they wear bathing suits.

The area we visited is a common vacation spot—a resort area where most people feel strangely at liberty to shed their clothes and boldly parade around in public wearing nothing more than what we refer to as "colored underwear."

While this was certainly not our idea of a *vacation*, we determined to enjoy each other, the weather, and the break from cell phones, computers, and school-work.

Birds of a Feather

Melissa and I were strolling through the hotel with Emma and Grace, my one- and two-year-old daughters, while my husband was in a meeting in one of the boardrooms. As we walked, we found ourselves repeatedly needing to cast our eyes downward to avoid almost constant visual assault.

Consider the following statements from the Westminster Assembly's Larger Catechism* **(Questions 137-139):**

❧ **Question 137**: Which is the seventh commandment?

- **Answer**: The seventh commandment is, Thou shalt not commit adultery.

❧ **Question 138**: What are the duties required in the seventh commandment?

- **Answer**: The duties required in the seventh commandment are, chastity in body, mind, affections, words, and behavior; and the preservation of it in ourselves and others; watchfulness over the eyes and all the senses; temperance, keeping of chaste company, *modesty in apparel*; marriage by those that have not the gift of continency, conjugal love, and cohabitation; diligent labor in our callings; shunning all occasions of uncleanness, and resisting temptations thereunto.

❧ **Question 139**: What are the sins forbidden in the seventh commandment?

- **Answer**: The sins forbidden in the seventh commandment, besides the neglect of the duties required, are, adultery, fornication, rape, incest, sodomy, and all unnatural lusts; all unclean imaginations, thoughts, purposes, and affections; all corrupt or filthy communications, or listening thereunto; wanton looks, impudent or light behavior, *immodest apparel*; prohibiting of lawful, and dispensing with unlawful marriages; allowing, tolerating, keeping of stews, and resorting to them; entangling vows of single life, undue delay of marriage; having more wives or husbands than one at the same time; unjust divorce, or desertion; idleness, gluttony, drunkenness, unchaste company; lascivious songs, books, pictures, dancings, stage plays; and all other provocations to, or acts of uncleanness, either in ourselves or others.

*A catechism is a form of instruction by means of questions and answers. *The Westminster Confession of Faith* and Shorter and Larger Catechisms were written in the 1640s by a group of 151 men: 10 Lords, 20 commoners, and 121 divines.

"Here comes another colorful flamingo!" Melissa warned, looking down. Sure enough, a pretentious young bird came strutting by us, and the poor thing seemed to have lost most of her feathers!

Blessed is he that watcheth, and keepeth his garments, lest he walk naked, and they see his shame. (Revelation 16:15)

Wishing to encourage my daughter, I pointed out the first long skirt I could find. I spoke too soon. My daughter shook her head, disappointed. "Mom, she may be wearing a long skirt, but she *walks* like she's wearing a *short* skirt."

She was right. Although the young lady was wearing a very long skirt, it was also very tight (her back side was distinctly outlined), and the exaggerated swing of her hips spoke even louder than what she was wearing.

A Heart Condition

Reflecting on the experience, we were aware that modesty is not only how much flesh we expose or what we choose to wear. It is also how we speak and how we carry ourselves. It truly is a condition of the heart (1 Peter 3:3-5).

While we don't know whether this young lady was a Christian or not, we do know that her demeanor and carriage did not reflect Christ. Regardless of the plumage she sported, her swagger said, "Look at me!" In fact, it distinctly invited, "Look at my tail feathers!" (Proverbs 7:10) It may not be what was on her mind, but it was what she was communicating to others, and I am certain that men walking behind her heard that message loud and clear.

You know the old saying, "Birds of a feather flock together"? Well, it's true! We are surrounded by a culture that glorifies self, vulgarity, sloppiness, and perversion. Though we are surrounded by this culture, we don't have to be immersed in it. We are not "of the same feather," so we shouldn't look as though we "flock together." At the very least, we can certainly make sure we have enough feathers to cover ourselves.

I counsel thee to buy of me gold tried in the fire, that thou mayest be rich; and white
raiment, that thou mayest be clothed, and that the shame of thy nakedness do not
appear. (Revelation 3:18)

May the Lord take your life and consecrate it to Himself. May your very presence in a room convict and turn hearts to Christ, bringing honor to your earthly father while glorifying your Father in Heaven.

Share Your Heart

- Have you ever thought about what you look like from behind—how tight or sheer your clothing is? Ask your mother to stand behind you and watch you walk. Ask her if she thinks you swing your hips or swagger.

- How is modesty a heart issue? Discuss ways that heart issues show up in our actions.

- When you walk up a flight of stairs, what do men behind you see? What types of clothing would be the most modest in this situation?

- Have you ever worn a long, flowing skirt or dress? How did it make you feel? How did others view you? Did it properly cover your private areas with no problem?

- Do you wear skirts that have slits that are cut higher than you would actually wear your skirt? What happens when you walk or sit? What happens on a windy day?

- Is your clothing modest to the people who are sitting behind you in church? Ask your mother or a wise female friend to stand behind you while you bend over to pick up a book. Now do the same with them standing in front of you. What did she see? What would your father think?

- Raise your hands high above your head. Does your tummy show? You may think, "I'll never be walking around with my hands above my

head," but this is a good all-around test. I've seen young ladies in blouses that seemed modest until they bent over to pick up a toddler or had to reach up high on a shelf.

◈ How low is your neckline? Look in the mirror while holding onto your knees. Do you see cleavage? If so, everyone else does too! If you are fuller in the chest area, you may need to be more careful of certain fabrics. Sweaters, knits, and the newer "stretchy" fabrics tend to cling and accentuate the bust line, and tops that are too large fall open easily.

◈ Be aware of where others' eyes may be drawn. You want them to look at your face, not other parts of your body, while they are talking to you. Avoid garments that hug areas which should be kept private.

◈ Would you feel naked wearing your nightgown or undergarments into a courtroom or church? What would your pastor and his wife think if you invited them over to supper, then answered the door in your underwear? Would they be shocked? Why do many of us think it is acceptable then to invite fellow Christians over for a pool party where everyone is wearing "colored underwear"? Discuss your answer with your mother (Romans 12:2).

◈ Tonight when you get ready for bed, stand alone in your underwear. Pretend that your undergarments are made of a stretchy, clingy fabric (like a bathing suit) and picture that they are colorful—maybe with a bright floral print. Now try to imagine walking outside of your room. Were you embarrassed at even the thought? How about walking to your neighbor's house?

◈ If your underwear is a bit skimpy, imagine adding just a few inches of fabric. Did that make it any better? Do you still have the urge to cover up? Discuss how we have been conditioned by the world to accept public nakedness, all in the name of recreation and fun—or even Christian *liberty*. How should we change our thinking? (1Peter 1:14)

∾ Talk about how someone can be dressed *modestly* from head to toe and still reveal an immodest demeanor.

∾ Read Proverbs 7:10-11 and Proverbs 31:22, 25).

∾ Look up the following words in the dictionary. Discuss with your mother how they might apply to immodesty:

- Conceit

- Haughtiness

- Egocentric

- Ostentatious

∾ What is the root sin of each of these offenses?

∾ Read all of Proverbs Chapter 7 and then read Matthew Henry's commentary on it below:

Of the person tempting, not a common prostitute, for she was a married wife (v. 19), and, for aught that appears, lived in reputation among her neighbours, not suspected of any such wickedness, and yet, in the twilight of the evening, when her husband was abroad, abominably impudent. She is here described, 1. By her dress. She had the attire of a harlot (v. 10), gaudy and flaunting, to set her off as a beauty; perhaps she was painted as Jezebel, and went with her neck and breasts bare, loose, and en disha-bille*. The purity of the heart will show itself in the modesty of the dress, which becomes women professing godliness. 2. By her craft and manage-ment. She is subtle of heart, mistress of all the arts of wheedling, and knowing how by all her caresses to serve her own base purposes. 3. By her temper and carriage. She is loud and stubborn, talkative and self-willed, noisy and troublesome, wilful and headstrong, all tongue, and will have her saying, right or wrong, impatient of check and control, and cannot bear to be counselled, much less reproved, by husband or parents, ministers or friends. She is a daughter of Belial, that will endure no yoke. 4. By her place, not her own house; she hates the confinement and employment of

---

* Partially dressed in a loose or careless manner.

that; her feet abide not there any longer than needs must. She is all for gadding abroad, changing place and company. Now is she without in the country, under pretence of taking the air, now in the streets of the city, under pretence of seeing how the market goes. She is here, and there, and every where but where she should be. She lies in wait at every corner, to pick up such as she can make a prey of. Virtue is a penance to those to whom home is a prison. (*Matthew Henry's* Commentary on the Whole Bible, New Modern Edition, Complete and Unabridged; Hendrickson Publishers, Inc., 1991, p. 679).

- Do you see what could be described as the "attire of a harlot" in the styles offered in most department stores today?
- What do you think is meant by "her feet abide not in her house?"
- Was the woman described in Proverbs 7 modest? Was she focused on serving her husband and her household faithfully or on gratifying herself?
- Men tend to sin by lusting after women, while women tend to sin by lusting to be lusted after. Lust is the very opposite of love because it *takes* instead of *gives*.
- If a maiden knowingly exposes private parts of her body or wears clothing that may incite lust in a young man, then she is acting selfishly. Again, this is the opposite of what Scripture describes as love. Do you think the Proverbs 7 woman loved the young man she enticed? Do you think she enjoyed flaunting her body? Have you ever chosen an outfit because you thought it might get the attention of a boy? Pray about your answer. Discuss the selfish motives behind choosing your wardrobe this way.

Charity suffereth long, and is kind; charity envieth not; charity vaunteth not itself, is not puffed up, Doth not behave itself unseemly, seeketh not her own, is not easily provoked, thinketh no evil; Rejoiceth not in iniquity, but rejoiceth in the truth; Beareth all things, believeth all things, hopeth all things, endureth all things. (1 Corinthians 13:4-7)

Are you dressing for the approval of man or God? Is your goal to impress or attract others or to be pleasing to God and to glorify Him? Be honest! After you discuss this chapter, spend some time praying together.

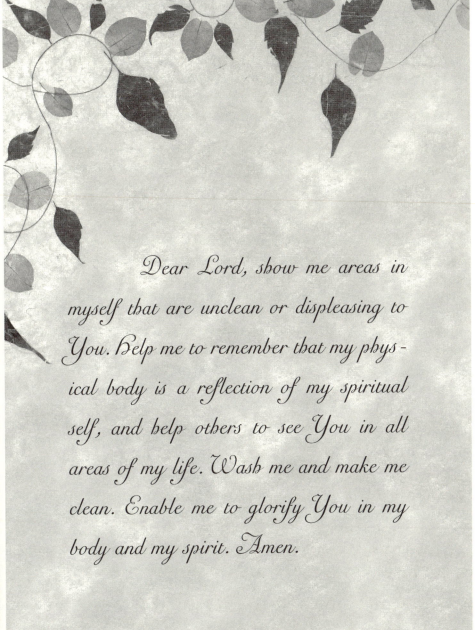

Dear Lord, show me areas in myself that are unclean or displeasing to You. Help me to remember that my physical body is a reflection of my spiritual self, and help others to see You in all areas of my life. Wash me and make me clean. Enable me to glorify You in my body and my spirit. Amen.

Chapter 14

THE BATH:

Powdered and Perfumed

Then will I sprinkle clean water upon you, and ye shall be clean: from all your filthiness, and from all your idols, will I cleanse you. (Ezekiel 36:25)

Bath time may be eagerly embraced by the active toddler as a joyous splash-fest of bubbles, toy boats, and squirting rubber fish, while a rough-and-tumble boy might wholeheartedly avoid soap and water as if they contained poisonous properties. A weary young mother may look forward to her steaming, perfumed bath at the end of the day with eager anticipation, while a busy father may shower quickly in the morning, viewing bath time as a simple necessity and nothing more. It's interesting how bath time can be perceived so differently by people of different personalities, ages, and sexes. Consider the following scene in our own home recently:

"Caleb, have you taken your bath?"

"Yes, Christa," my seven-year-old charmer proudly answered his nineteen-year-old sister.

"Really? Are you sure?" she answered, not convinced of the thoroughness of tonight's record-time bath.

"Yes, Do you want to smell me?" he chirped, ready to give her a good whiff.

"No, thank you, Caleb, aftershave isn't what I was hoping to smell—*that* I can smell from here. Did you use soap?"

"Um, not *much*," he answered, a bit deflated.

Before she could reply, he was heading back up the stairs prepared for a *real* bath—one that actually involved soap touching his body.

My powdered and perfumed young maiden couldn't control the urge: "Scrub your body. Shampoo your hair—with shampoo. And use a *washcloth*! Use lots of soap, and don't forget to wash your ears—inside and out! And use warm water— it's not a swimming pool. And if you don't do a good job this time—*I'll* bathe you myself!"

At that, we heard him scamper quickly into the bathroom and shut the door tight! Ah . . . little brothers!

Someone Stinky This Way Comes

Unfortunately, the battle over the bathtub isn't always waged between big sisters and little boys in love with mud puddles. Sometimes girls and even adults, both men and women, have the same trouble with healthy hygiene and cleanliness.

My husband and I once attended a church with a man who had truly offensive body odor. He came to church in filthy clothes, greasy hair, and he smelled—bad. You could see the pained expression on the faces of the poor souls who were stuck sitting beside him during service.

We knew him personally, and he was not ill or handicapped in any way. In fact, other than his grooming habits, he was a fairly strong Christian. Unfortunately, he earned a reputation for not being very pleasant to be around, simply because of his apparent refusal to take care of his physical body. I always wondered what it would have been like to see him with a decent haircut, clean clothes, and without the fog of two-week-old perspiration engulfing his body.

I have also known married women who attend church or social gatherings with greasy hair, a disheveled appearance, and no apparent attempt to look or smell nice for their husbands. They most likely developed poor grooming habits as young maidens and failed to honor their family or others by paying attention to their outward presentation.

Whether a casual or formal occasion and whether you're rich, poor, young, or old, neatness and cleanliness are almost always possible. But does God really care whether or not we are neat and clean?

Some people have a **Gnostic** view of the flesh and suppose that the way we present ourselves to others physically doesn't matter. They believe that our physical bodies are evil and since we are spiritual beings God only cares about our hearts.

James 2:1-4 warns us of our sinful tendency toward partiality of those who are richer, dress nicer, are more beautiful, smarter, or have a higher rank in society. We are not to be respecters of persons. Scripture teaches us to treat others the way we wish to be treated, to love our neighbors as ourselves, and to prefer others over ourselves (Romans 12:10).Grooming ourselves, cleansing our bodies, and presenting ourselves to others in a comely way, is all part of loving our neighbor as well as glorifying God.

Of course God is concerned about our spiritual well-being (Romans 6:12, 1 Corinthians 6:13-20), but He is concerned about our physical bodies as well (Ruth 3:3, Hebrews 10:22). He made us physical beings as well as spiritual, and He has given us instructions on how to conduct ourselves and take care of both.

Matthew urged even believers who were fasting to wash and groom themselves, so they would appear refreshed and joyful, not somber and gloomy (Matthew 6:17).

A Sweet Scent

Ointment and perfume rejoice the heart: so doth the sweetness of a man's friend by hearty counsel. (Proverbs 27:9)

A young maiden should develop good grooming habits. She will be pleasing to God and to others now, and when she is grown and married she will be a blessing to her husband and children as well. Cleanliness, neatness, and a bright countenance will become habits that are effortless and part of her very personality.

For as long as I can remember, my mother enjoyed taking hot baths in the evenings. I have tried to follow her example and take time in the evening for a quiet retreat with scented bubbles or bath salts. Sometimes I simply use a few drops of various essential oils. As my precious husband and children bless me on birthdays and Mother's Day with special gifts, I indulge in the use of scented bath powders and light perfumes.

Aside from my regular morning shower, I admit I don't always have time for more than a quick sponge bath and fluff of scented powder at night. But when it's possible, not only is a nice bath a relaxing treat for me, it is a blessing to my husband and children as well. When my husband retires for the night, he is greeted by the smell of lavender, rose, sandalwood, or ylang-ylang!

For the longest time, my youngest son thought I naturally smelled of lavender. When I rocked him at night, he even buried his nose in the collar of my robe and took a deep sniff. Somehow it created a meaningful memory for him, and he now recognizes this scent as distinctively feminine and pleasant.

Likewise, my daughters love to smell good. Even the toddlers love for us to put a few drops of lavender oil and a cap full of bubbles into their bath. After they are properly scrubbed, powdered, and dressed, they go through the routine of getting big hugs, kisses, and a good "sniff" from Daddy. He typically throws his head back and dramatically extols the merit of their intoxicating flowery aroma. Then they giggle and run to have a brother or sister smell them next. This is one of the highlights of our pre-bedtime routine and a wonderful way to begin a good habit of feminine cleanliness.

A disciplined habit of washing and grooming ourselves is one way we can glorify God. Pray and ask God to reveal His Word to you as you seek to learn the importance of cleanliness and good grooming habits.

Share Your Heart

> ✤ Look up and discuss the definition of the word *Gnostic* with your mother. How could Gnostic thinking affect the way we view purity.

❧ Read 2 Corinthians 7:1. Discuss how cleansing the body is one part of "perfecting holiness" in the fear of God.

❧ Read Ephesians 5:27. What kind of church is God perfecting to present to Christ as His bride? What can this verse tell us about God's opinion of presenting ourselves to our husbands?

❧ Read Revelation 19:8. What is the fine linen likened to? Are the terms *white* and *clean* meant to symbolize holiness or evil? Why do you think so?

❧ Discuss ways that physical cleanliness can be an *outward* sign of *inward* purity.

❧ Read and discuss Ezekiel 36:25. To what does "your filthiness" refer in this verse? What physical element does Scripture use to symbolize cleansing, and from what is God cleansing us? How do you think this might be significant as we discuss the importance of washing our physical bodies?

❧ When discussing filthiness, Scripture seems to always admonish us to put it far away from us. God also explains how He will cleanse us from filthiness (sin). God's Word doesn't seem to have anything good to say about filthiness. Why do you think God compares sin to filthiness?

❧ Read 1 Corinthians 6:20. In what two ways does Paul direct us to glorify God in this verse? In what ways could neglecting to bathe and groom our bodies bring dishonor to the name of Christ?

❧ What are some common sins that could cause someone to neglect habits of cleanliness or good grooming, including regular hair washing and brushing, dental hygiene, and the washing or maintenance of her clothing?

❧ Should *every* act of physical uncleanness be considered sin? Why or why not?

❧ Is the evidence of meticulous cleanliness sure proof of godliness? (Matthew 23:27)

ᔐ Read Matthew 6:17. How does Matthew's admonition about cleanliness relate to modesty (not drawing attention to one's self)? Why do you think people might be tempted to neglect bathing or grooming themselves on days when they are fasting?

ᔐ Read and discuss Exodus 19:10. Why were God's people required to maintain outward actions of bodily cleanliness? What were they preparing for? What might the Israelites have been pondering in their minds as they washed their clothes? What did this act of cleanliness symbolize?

ᔐ Men see our clothes, but God sees our hearts. Why would it matter to God if we did not wash our clothes?

ᔐ How much good will it do us if we take special care in making our bodies clean but our hearts and lives remain full of filth and indulgence? (Matthew 23:25-26, Isaiah 1:16)

ᔐ Ask God to show you the areas in your life that are unclean or impure. Repent of these things, and ask Him to cleanse you in every area of your life (Psalm 51:10, 1 Peter 3:21).

ᔐ If you haven't been in the habit of keeping yourself as clean as you should, ask God to help you. Ask your mother to keep you accountable. If you need it, keep a daily checklist.

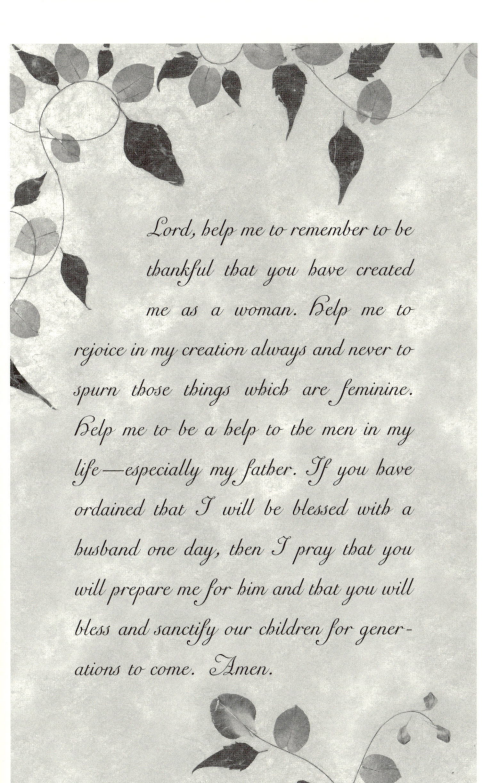

Lord, help me to remember to be thankful that you have created me as a woman. Help me to rejoice in my creation always and never to spurn those things which are feminine. Help me to be a help to the men in my life—especially my father. If you have ordained that I will be blessed with a husband one day, then I pray that you will prepare me for him and that you will bless and sanctify our children for generations to come. Amen.

Chapter 15

A KNIGHT IN
SHINING ARMOR

Likewise, ye husbands, dwell with them according to knowledge, giving honour unto the wife, as unto the weaker vessel, and as being heirs together of the grace of life; that your prayers be not hindered (1 Peter 3:7).

E very little girl dreams of being a princess—especially one who is rescued by a daring and valiant prince! Something in the female design relishes the thought of being cherished and protected by a man—first by her father and later by her beloved husband. This is evident in the way a daughter's eyes light up when Daddy says she's pretty and the way a young bride's heart skips a beat because her enamored husband fawns over her, insisting on carrying the "heavy things"—the same heavy things she managed to carry just fine before they met. It is in the face of an older woman who smiles at a young man who opens the door for her—a disappearing practice.

Unfortunately it is no longer politically correct to hope for such things. In fact, a feminist may glare at a man who would dare open a door for her. After all, she is just as strong and capable as a man! She has the *right* to open her own door, thank you very much! No wonder many men are now saying, "Alright, then, get your own door!" Unfortunately feminism has given us a few other "*liberating*" gifts as well.

A Maiden's Warfare

by Carol A. DeLadurantey

Press on to heights of glory now,
And keep thou steady eye.

One must not falter in this fight,
Though some may flee or fly.

Take hold the charge thou hast been given,
To battle we must go.

But not with our own maiden hands
Do we take up shield or bow.

We wage this war in words and actions,
With our every deed.

We follow Christ our captain,
Thro' him we will succeed.

Tell me now have we forgot
The charge from God above

To keep our hearts in purity, grace,
Modesty, truth and love.

These are our weapons, our shields, our swords;
In this battle we now fight.

We strive not for an earthly king,
But for our God of truth and might!

Where Have All the Knights Gone?

It is no longer unusual for a mother to allow virtual strangers to feed, nurture, and train her infant while she heads off to a self-promoting career. Sometimes the father is left home to tend to the little ones and applauded for becoming a "Mr. Mom." Roles are reversed, and everyone cheers.

In our time women are encouraged to be bold, roaring leaders. Now young maidens even have the "right" to go to battle to protect and die for perfectly strong and able grown men who choose not to serve their country—or in some cases, even work an honest job. Young maidens are given equal opportunity to crouch in muddy ditches, shoulder to shoulder, sweating and bleeding alongside "fellow" soldiers in combat. Equal opportunity just might end if she finds herself captured by the enemy, but we're not supposed to think about that.

Mothers who should be home nursing and cuddling their infants are tearfully handing their blessings over to family members and friends, donning fatigues and combat boots (Deuteronomy 22:5) and heading off to war—possibly never to return. Why aren't the men protecting the women? (Numbers 1:2-4, Deuteronomy 20:8). Why are little girls fighting wars while able-bodied men shamefully sit in their recliners watching them on television? Where have all the knights in shining armor gone? That's easy—in many cases the maidens told them to hit the road! Sinfully they obeyed.

Behold, thy people in the midst of thee are women: the gates of thy land shall be set wide open unto thine enemies: the fire shall devour thy bars. (Nahum 3:13)

A Maiden Is as a Maiden Does

It is interesting to watch people in our community respond to my older daughters. Instead of being viewed as "chicks," they are considered young ladies. My older daughters carry themselves with dignity as they help with younger siblings while out in public, so many times strangers assume they are much older than they really are. Folks expect girls in their teens to be clad in loud, trendy clothes, wearing revealing styles, and presenting sloppy demeanors. As a result, they are confused when they see soft flowing skirts and modest embroidered blouses on ones so young—they assume my girls must simply be very young-looking grown women.

Just like Grandma used to say, "If you act like a lady, you'll be treated like one." This is a true statement and can be said of maidenhood as well. If you act like a maiden, you can expect to be treated like one. Likewise, if you act like a harlot, you can be certain there will be those who are more than willing to treat you like one. Furthermore, if you act like a man, you just may get what you ask for.

We do live in a fallen world, and many virginal maidens have, in fact, been treated like harlots through no fault of their own. Similarly, many harlots who did not deserve honor have been treated with great respect by well-trained Christian gentlemen, but the general principle still applies that you will most likely be treated according to how you present yourself.

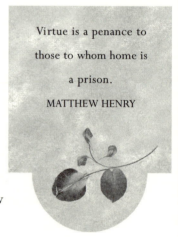

Virtue is a penance to those to whom home is a prison.

MATTHEW HENRY

What we desperately need is a return to chivalry and godly maidenhood. Many young ladies are convinced that if they don't act "cool" or if they fail to dress like "everyone else" then they will be teased. Some girls suppose it makes them more attractive to display "toughness," even acting loud and boisterous in an attempt to draw attention.

Godly young men who are ready for marriage are desperately searching for true maidens of virtue. Therefore, if young women would put away their immodest ways and seek virtuous, feminine loveliness, I believe they would be surprised by the respectful treatment they would naturally receive. True men of honor are absolutely enchanted by true, godly, feminine beauty—not the type that comes from a tube of lipstick, but the kind that comes from a meek and quiet spirit. Once a godly knight finds a true maiden of virtue, he may also find himself with the urge to slay a dragon or two on her behalf!

Share Your Heart

- ✎ Do you think a man should open a door for a woman? Why? When a boy or man opens a door for you, how do you react? Do you walk through and say, "Thank you," or do you take the door from him in embarrassment? Discuss your answer.

- ✎ Read Isaiah 3:11-14. What do you think these verses mean? How do you think they might apply to us today? Discuss this with your mother.

- ✎ Read Proverbs 9:13. What kind of woman does Scripture describe as clamorous? What does the word *clamorous* mean? Can you ever be described this way? Discuss with your mother ways you can avoid this type of behavior.

- ✎ Read Proverbs 21:9-19. Do you know girls who are pushy and loud? What about those who seem to always be angry or picking a fight? How do other people respond to them?

- ✎ Read 2 Corinthians 11:2. God plans to present the Bride (the Church) as a spotless and chaste virgin to His Son, Jesus Christ. This is a perfect picture of marriage. What kind of example does this give you in remaining pure for your future husband? What model does this give your father?

- ✎ Read 1 Peter 3:7 and then answer the following questions:

- ✎ What do you think "the weaker vessel" means? How do you like being described this way? Mother, describe how you may have struggled with this Scripture in the past.

- ✎ Is stating that women are the "weaker vessel" meant to be an insult to women or a holy protection of them?

- ✎ Do you feel that women today are honored, cherished, and protected? Why or why not?

> Read Proverbs 31:10-31 aloud with your mother. Note the key characteristics of a virtuous woman.

> Discuss with your mother how your present obedience to your father will directly relate to your submission to your husband later. Mother, talk about the difficulties many women have in submitting to their husbands. Share your own struggles in this area.

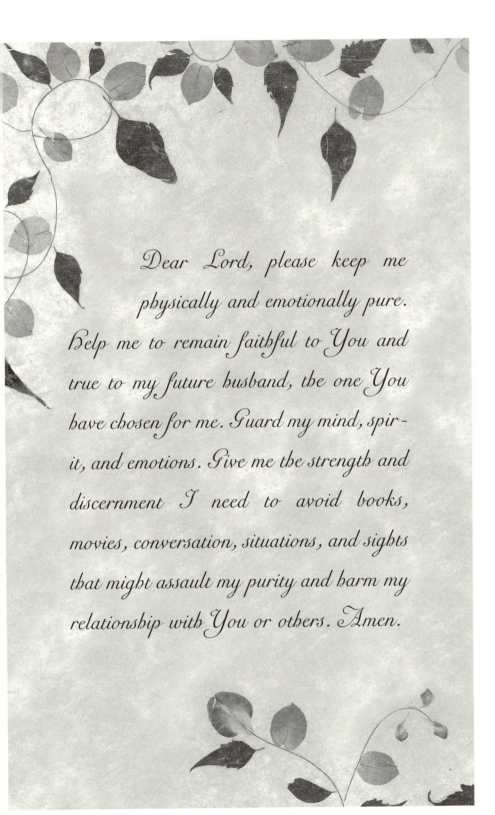

Dear Lord, please keep me physically and emotionally pure. Help me to remain faithful to You and true to my future husband, the one You have chosen for me. Guard my mind, spirit, and emotions. Give me the strength and discernment I need to avoid books, movies, conversation, situations, and sights that might assault my purity and harm my relationship with You or others. Amen.

Chapter 16

DELAYED AWAKENINGS

I adjure you, O daughters of Jerusalem, by the gazelles or the does of the field, that you not stir up or awaken love until it pleases. (Song of Solomon 2:7)

The cover of the book looked harmless enough: a peaceful farm, wildflowers bordering a trickling brook, a young girl—the very picture of innocence—daydreaming on the porch . . . and in the background, a very handsome young man with a wistful expression, leaning against the fence post.

"Why can't I read it, Mom?" Sarah asked, puzzled. "There are no curse words, no indecent behavior, and no violence in the whole book! It was recommended by my friend at church, and Grandma bought it for me. It's a *Christian* book! Please, can I read it?"

Sarah's mother sighed. How could she explain to Sarah the powerful emotions that romance novels could stir in her young heart? Browsing the pages of this popular new novel, Sarah's mother noticed more problems than just a poorly written story.

"Sarah, you're going to have to trust me. As women, we are created to desire a husband. It's natural, and there is nothing more wonderful than being eager to walk in the role for which you are designed—to be a wife and mother. But if certain yearnings are awakened too early they can cause all kinds of temptations and trouble. You will find yourself battling thoughts that might never even have occurred to you otherwise—at least not with the same power and frequency."

Sarah knew her mother was right. She had paged through the second chapter and been drawn into the story of boy-meets-girl. She remembered reading the back of the book and seeing the picture of the young man on the front cover. Even that small sampling had given her butterflies in her stomach and made her think about how much the boy on the cover looked like Joshua at church. It had even stirred thoughts of whether or not *he* might be *the one*. Still, she couldn't help being disappointed by not being allowed to read the book.

Sarah's mother went on, "As you know, we are planning for you to marry within a protected courtship setting. Part of our responsibility to God and to you is to guard your purity and insure that you are faithful to your future husband even now. Did you know that the choices you make now will affect your marriage to your husband later?"

"No, Ma'am," Sarah whispered. She had never considered that her future husband might not want her reading romantic stories!

"Just as physical purity is important, being faithful to your future husband also means remaining true to him *emotionally*—even before you are married. Emotional purity involves saving your romantic feelings for your husband. You will be able to offer him your whole heart on your wedding day—not just the bits and pieces that are left.

"Furthermore, in the unlikely event that God will call you to singleness, it is even more vital that you guard your heart and not be consumed with something God may not have for you.

"It's also good to be careful not to fantasize about a 'perfect husband.' As much in love as you will be on your wedding day, you will still discover—as every married woman has—that you have married a real man, not a fictitious hero. Real men can never measure up to the men in romance novels. Hebrews 13:5 tells us to let our conversation be without covetousness and to be content with such things as we have."

Sarah thought about the book again. It was just a book—she wasn't having a conversation about any young man. Then the rest of the verse pricked her conscience . . . the part about contentment came to mind.

As if her mother read her thoughts, she said, "Should this apply to our recreation as well as our conversation? As a single young woman who is guarding her heart and focusing her attentions on serving God and preparing for her future, do you really want to read something that would possibly stir untimely emotions or even immoral thoughts and temptations? Do you understand what I am saying?" (Proverbs 13:12)

Sarah nodded. She knew her mother was making sense, and more than that, she knew her mother only had her best interest in mind. She had learned long ago that her parents took their responsibility in training her for the Lord very seriously, and she could trust that their decisions were wisely considered, with much prayer and thought.

Sarah's mother took her daughter's hands in her own. "Sarah, marriage is a precious and beautiful gift from God. That strong desire must be kept dormant for now. It comes not only from simmering hormones, but also from the excitement of knowing you are nearing a fresh season of life—a season that includes beginning a new role as a wife and mother.

"That stirring—that God-given desire that I referred to—when properly reined within a godly marriage, is a breathtaking and unmatched gift of God. Be patient and focus on preparing yourself. So many young women, even if they remain physically pure, waste their girlhood in discontent—yearning for romance and foolishly fawning over every boy they see.

"But you, my daughter, will be well prepared for your groom when he comes. He will find you well-equipped for your position as his honored helpmate with your lantern filled, radiating purity. You will ease into motherhood with confidence, grace, and an eager desire to serve. And if you continue in your diligence serving here at home, you will be a much more organized and prepared homemaker than I was!"

Sarah saw the tears in her mother's eyes. She realized that she could trust her mother's judgment and that she could believe in her mother's genuine love for her. She also remembered that even when she didn't agree with a particular decision her parents made, if she trusted God and His loving choice of working through her parents, He would use her obedience to work everything out for her ultimate good.

She knew that God always showed Himself faithful. She would remain content and trusting knowing that the sweet fruit of both would be well worth it.

Share Your Heart

- Have you ever read a book that made you feel discontent or restless? Was it hard to get out of your mind? How did you finally resolve it?

- What other problems could books or movies with a strong "romantic" focus cause?

- Have you ever thought about or talked to a boy and felt "butterflies" in your stomach? Sometimes hormones and a changing/growing body fool us into believing we are "in love." Discuss these feelings with your mother. Discuss why God gave us hormones. How can those "stirrings" be a great blessing within marriage?

- How would you have reacted to the "no" answer Sarah received from her mother about reading the book?

- Share a time when you disagreed with a decision your parents made for you. How did you handle it? Did you trust God and obey, or rebel and do things your way? What was the final result? How might things have turned out if you had chosen differently?

- How could fantasizing about boys you know, perhaps wondering if they are God's choice for you as a husband, be dangerous? How could it turn into a case of being emotionally unfaithful to your future husband? How would you feel if you knew your future husband was thinking in this same manner about girls he knows, right now?

❧ Are you "content with such things as you have?" (Hebrews 13:5) Will you be content if God calls you to singleness? In what ways do you struggle with contentment?

❧ Do you find yourself coveting the lives of those who are married? Share your struggles with your mother. Are you struggling with your womanly role by wishing for independence, are you jealous of those who seem to have more fun and exciting lives than you, are you obsessing about a door God has not opened in your life? If you have been coveting in any of these ways, repent and ask your mother to pray for you. Ask God to give you a contented and trusting spirit.

❧ Read and discuss the following Scriptures:

- Psalm 130:5
- Hebrews 10:36

❧ What are some practical ways you can guard your heart?

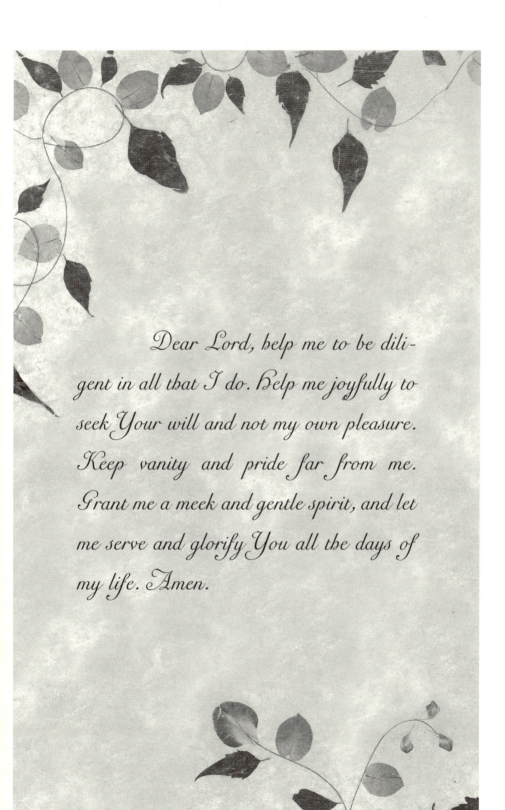

Dear Lord, help me to be diligent in all that I do. Help me joyfully to seek Your will and not my own pleasure. Keep vanity and pride far from me. Grant me a meek and gentle spirit, and let me serve and glorify You all the days of my life. Amen.

Chapter 17

LADY OF LEISURE

*By this time her old disposition had begun to rouse again. She had been doing her duty,
and had in consequence begun again to think herself Somebody. However strange it may
well seem, to do one's duty will make any one conceited who only does it sometimes. Those
who do it always would as soon think of being conceited of eating their dinner as of doing
their duty. What honest boy would pride himself on not picking pockets? A thief who was
trying to reform would. To be conceited of doing one's duty is then a sign of how little one
does it, and how little one sees what a contemptible thing it is not to do it. Could any but a
low creature be conceited of not being contemptible? Until our duty becomes to us common
as breathing, we are poor creatures. (The Wise Woman by George MacDonald,
Straban & Co., London, 1875)*

*A*shley lay in the hammock watching the clouds wander by like
nomadic wisps of smoke. The air was clean and fresh on her skin
as she swayed back and forth between the trees. She set her book
aside and closed her eyes, lazily listening to the leaves banter back and forth. In her
reverie she dreamily fancied herself as the beautiful heroine in the novel she had
been reading.

Ashley was three years older than her nineteen-year-old sister, Emmaline, but
everyone thought Emmaline was the eldest. Ashley presumed it was because
Emmaline was taller. "She can have the height," Ashley thought with satisfaction.
Though Emmaline was pretty in her own way, Ashley was the striking one—the
"jewel of the crown," she had unfortunately heard someone say. Rachel, just twelve
years old and the youngest child of the family, was every bit as tall as Emmaline
and almost as industrious.

The book Ashley had been reading lay clumsily in her lap. "The whole story is beginning to drag," she thought. She turned to notice her mother and sisters busily sowing seeds into the fertile soil behind their barn. She decided to go into the house to finish the chapter. Ashley determined that her sisters must have begun the gardening at that particular moment in an attempt to make her feel guilty—but no matter, she wasn't going to let them spoil her day!

Ashley entered the kitchen and poured herself a glass of cool lemonade. The warm day made the lemonade taste even sweeter. She considered taking lemonade to her mother and sisters. "That would be nice of me," she thought. So she pulled out the large serving tray from under the hutch and filled the glasses full.

Welcoming smiles greeted her as she met her mother and sisters in the garden. "Thank you Ashley," Emmaline said gratefully. "What a thoughtful thing to do!" The rest of the women agreed.

The shadow of guilt she felt from not helping in the garden didn't subside, but Ashley offered a painted smile, along with a sugary "You're welcome" in return.

Ashley dashed up the stairs to finish her book before anyone could ask her to help with dinner. "If you give them an inch, they'll take a mile," she thought, trying to content herself with her latest good deed.

As she was just getting comfortable on her lavishly cushioned daybed, she heard the doorbell ring. She wondered if anyone would hear the bell from the garden. Finally, after the third ring, she realized she was going to have to put her book down and answer the door herself.

When she reached the door, a young man was just turning to leave. He looked familiar. Curiously, she opened the door and offered an apology for taking so long in getting to the door. "Today has been *so* busy; we didn't even hear the bell. So sorry to keep you waiting." She smiled coyly.

"I'm sorry to disturb you, Ma'am," he said politely. "I'm looking for Mr. Johnson."

"Do you have business with him?" she asked.

"Well, yes, he hired me to work on his property for the summer. I believe I have the right place—is this the Johnson farm?"

She looketh well to the ways of her household,
and eateth not the bread of idleness.
~ Proverbs 31:27 ~

"That's us!" she confirmed. "Mr. Johnson is my father. Come in. I'll get my mother."

Ashley fetched her mother and sisters, and they all managed to make the stranger feel welcome and quite at home.

His name was Louis, and he was the son of the widow that Mama knew in the next county. He would be working for Daddy for the summer in exchange for training on the farm, including the heavy equipment Daddy owned.

Louis had inherited a large farm from his father, and his mother was an invalid who needed his support. This summer arrangement could benefit both families. Daddy had known Louis's father and was a bit startled to see the remarkable resemblance in the boy's face.

As time passed, Louis seemed to become part of the family. He learned the routines and enthusiastically pitched in to help with the chores. Ashley felt obligated to help more than usual, just so she wouldn't be embarrassed by her own marked idleness. After a while, though, her concern wore off, and she was back to her normal routine—of lounging.

During dinner one night Daddy asked the girls how their day had been. Ashley told her father about her service to her mother and sisters. "I made sure everyone had a wonderful lunch today. I fixed a nice salad and even washed all the dishes." In her heart she was trying to ease her conscience again, since in reality she had spent her day avoiding work and focusing on her own pleasures.

"Wonderful! What about you, Rachel? How was your day?" Daddy asked, turning to his youngest daughter.

"I had a good day, Daddy," Rachel chirped. "I think I finally figured out how to keep the birds away from our tomatoes. If we put a red glass Christmas ornament on each plant, it fools them! They think it's a shiny tomato and try to eat it," the girl said cleverly.

"I guess that would deter those pesky birds! It sounds like we have a plan, Rachel," Daddy said proudly.

"Emmaline, tell Daddy about *your* day!" Rachel giggled.

"Oh, Daddy! What a day! The McLeods' cow escaped and wound up on our property. It was the funniest thing. She had wandered past the Millers' yard on her way to ours and passed under their clothesline. She showed up wearing Mrs. Miller's bright pink apron on her head!"

The whole table erupted with laughter. Louis added that he had seen Emmaline busy watering the flower garden. When he heard her shout that Daisy was loose and wearing a pink apron, he had rushed to help. "I must admit," he teased, "I wondered which daisy she was watering that was desperate enough to escape in a pink apron!" Again, everyone laughed.

"I really didn't mind," Ashley said, self-absorbed.

Everyone looked at Ashley, confused. "You didn't mind what?" Daddy said.

"Preparing lunch for everyone," she said, somewhat annoyed. "I was just telling you about it. It was no trouble at all, and I did all the dishes quickly" (Proverbs 26:16).

There was an uncomfortable silence in the room. "Yes, thank you for lunch, Ashley," Louis said as he excused himself from the table and went outside to put his tools away.

In truth, Rachel and Emmaline had washed and chopped the vegetables for the salad that morning, so all Ashley had to do was dump everything into the salad bowl and ring the dinner bell—since her sisters were outside working. They had used paper plates and plastic forks, so there weren't any dishes to speak of besides their glasses, which had been soaking in the sink when Mama came in to prepare dinner.

"Ashley, dear," Mama said, "please don't boast. You spent the majority of your day idle. I am going to make a list of chores for you to do tomorrow—and each day. Maybe then you will not feel the need to brag when you do some small thing." Insulted, Ashley excused herself for the night (Proverbs 13:1).

The next morning Ashley ignored the list Mama put on the refrigerator and curled up by the window to enjoy a bowl of strawberries and read another chapter of her book. Mama would be in town today visiting Louis's mother and helping to clean her house and prepare some meals for freezing. Ashley, still offended by her mother's words the previous night, decided she would claim forgetfulness and worry about the chores the next day.

Ashley wasn't sure how much time had passed and didn't even notice Louis walk in the side door. She jumped when he turned on the kitchen faucet. "Great day!" Louis said cheerfully, scrubbing the grease from his hands.

"Oh . . . yes," Ashley replied, dazed. Just then, Emmaline and Rachel entered the kitchen, red-faced and wet with perspiration. They were laughing, covered in soil, and looked a mess. They had been cleaning out the chicken coop. Amused, Louis stepped aside to let the ladies use the sink. Ashley smiled sweetly and handed Louis a towel. She was very glad he had not seen *her* disheveled and dirty.

Later that night, after everyone was in bed, Ashley began to daydream. She started to wonder why it was that Louis had come to the farm. Was he really training with her father, or was it just an excuse to see *her*? She had never dared to think such a thing before, but as she considered her latest novel, a romantic dream began to emerge.

Ashley freely indulged her fantasy until she was convinced that Louis was here to evaluate her as a potential wife. She could almost hear him asking her father for her hand. . . "Mr. Johnson, your daughter is so absolutely beautiful that I can hardly stand it. Please let me marry her, or I shall surely die!" Pulling her pillow over her face, she fell back on the bed dreamily.

The next morning Ashley woke late to the smell of eggs and fresh sausage downstairs. Emmaline had made her special homemade buttermilk biscuits, and strong coffee was brewing. "I wonder if everyone is up," Ashley thought. She would have been more honest with herself to think, "I wonder if a certain young man is up." Oddly enough, she didn't allow herself that luxury. She would rather think it was *he* who was wondering about *her*.

Ashley dressed herself and hurried downstairs, hoping her mother was not too upset with her for the undone chores. Upon entering the kitchen, she found her sisters talking at the kitchen table in a somber mood. From their expressions, she wondered if something awful had happened. "Is somebody sick? Did Mama make it home alright last night?" Ashley asked, alarmed.

"Mama is fine," Rachel said. It's just that she and Daddy have been in the study with Louis for a long time. We're wondering if something is wrong with Louis's mother. I know it's been more difficult for her since he's been away from home."

Ashley's spirit leapt. Alone. . .with Mama and Daddy? "I knew it!" she thought. "He must be asking for my hand in marriage this moment!"

She smiled as she recalled the clever ways she had made excuses to avoid the various chores—especially the dirty jobs. It's a good thing, too! She always made sure her hair was brushed and styled, her clothes were becoming, and her make-up was perfect. Fortunately he had never seen her looking dirty and smelly . . . like her sisters. Who knows what he would have thought of her! Casually she ran her fingers through her long hair with a smile. Her suppressed guilt hardly troubled her now.

The doorknob turned, and all three girls jumped. Mama emerged from the room with freshly wiped tears. "What happened, Mama? Is everything okay?" Rachel asked, almost in tears herself.

"Everything is absolutely fine, honey." Mama let out a half-laugh, half-sob and covered her mouth with her hand.

"What is it, Mother?" Emmaline asked, rushing to her mother's side.

Mother laughed more heartily now. "Don't worry child, I'm just thankful to the Lord. Come with me. I need to speak with you privately." Mother led Emmaline into the sunroom.

Ashley's mind was racing. What in the world was going on? Why was Mother having a private discussion with *Emmaline*? What was this all about? Why hadn't Daddy and Louis left the other room?

Rachel covered the biscuits and put them into the oven to keep warm. She turned to ask her sister if she would take care of the sausage and eggs while Rachel finished setting the table, but she discovered Ashley had vanished. Rachel sighed, accustomed to her oldest sister's poor work ethic.

Ashley settled herself into the rocker in the den near the air duct. While reading in this spot last summer, she had accidentally discovered that she could hear conversations taking place in the sunroom. It seemed that might come in handy today!

Ashley could hear her mother's tender voice. "Emmaline, dear, Daddy asked me to talk to you privately before bringing you into the study with Louis and him. Honey, Louis told your father and me that he wants you to be his wife! He has been impressed with your godliness, your feminine loveliness, your contented and obedient spirit, and the way you are not afraid of working hard to serve your family and God!" (Proverbs 31:27-31)

Dizzy with rage, Ashley thought for a moment that she would faint. Impossible! It can't be! Her heart raced, and nausea almost overtook her (Proverbs 13:4) How could she have been so foolish? Her head was spinning and tears burned her cheeks. Gradually her fury reduced to a low simmer, and reality slowly began to dawn on her.

Louis had not been impressed with her at all. In his eyes, her beauty was only skin deep. He was a godly man, and he wanted a woman of true worth who loved and feared the Lord. At that moment, the realization of her sin—her foolish vanity, her laziness, her self-centeredness, and her dishonesty—were set before her eyes in stark ugliness. The realization that she was the eldest and should have been the one setting a godly example caused her to wince. Conviction shot through her soul, and she felt real shame for the first time.

Ashley knew that a truly godly man would never be interested in such a selfish girl as herself. She shuddered when she considered the kind of man that *would* be attracted to someone like her. . . but at that moment, she wasn't concerned about acquiring a husband. Ashley's only concern was the empty pit in which she had found herself. Suddenly she saw the fictitious heroines in the novels she read as the shallow, evildoers that they were. How could she have wanted to fashion her life after such superficiality and wickedness?

In her despair, she felt the irresistible tug of the Holy Spirit upon her heart.

Repentance, like a searing fire, followed. Ashley knew she had no choice. In her misery, Ashley found joy; in her shame, she found peace; in her Savior, she found forgiveness and restoration (Jeremiah 31:19).

Share Your Heart

- ❧ How could Ashley's view of herself in the beginning have hindered her walk with the Lord? (Jeremiah 13:15)

- ❧ How could Ashley's reading choices have contributed to her fantasy life?

- ❧ Why do you think Ashley bragged about her small "acts of service" to her family? Were they genuine acts of service?

- ❧ What caused Ashley to feel insulted when her mother rebuked her? (Proverbs 15:20) Have you ever become quiet and sullen when your mother or father has corrected you? Have you ever responded to your parents' rebuke in your mind with words you never would have dared voice out loud—words that would have proved you had not accepted correction? Does this make you wise or foolish, according to Scripture? (Proverbs 9:8-9, 15:5)

- ❧ Do you think Ashley felt guilty about her laziness? Why or why not? Have you ever tried to cause others to focus on your "good deeds" so that they would not notice the areas where you were lacking?

- ❧ Discuss the differences in the three daughters' responses to their father's inquiry about their day. What made Ashley's so markedly different?

- ❧ What made Ashley finally repent? Sometimes conviction is painful, but the results are sweet. Take time to pray and thank God for those painful times of conviction and for His drawing you into repentance. Ask Him always to keep you close to Him this way. (Read Isaiah 55:6-7.)

Lord, give me a heart that is pure, one that will trust my father because I trust You. Guard my heart from the stranger, and keep it safe for my beloved. Grant my father wisdom and discernment, and help me to be obedient, patient, and faithful. Amen.

THE HEART OF A MAIDEN

And he shall turn the heart of the fathers to the children, and the heart of the children to their fathers, lest I come and smite the earth with a curse. (Malachi 4:6)

T he house was still dark as my sisters and I crept quietly down the stairs. Mama lit the candles on the mantle and turned on soft music. After just a few hours of sleep, the stillness of the morning made it seem as though we were dreaming. We gathered on the sofas and waited for Daddy to sit in "his spot" next to Mama.

Christa brought Daddy his steaming cup of gourmet coffee—black, just the way he likes it. I handed Mama hers, rich and creamy with too much sugar—perfect. We all sat for a moment enjoying each other's company and sipping coffee. Suddenly, we heard a faint squeal from the baby's room. Melissa jumped up to get little Emma and reappeared a moment later with a smiling bundle of cuddles and coos. She handed her to Mama to nurse.

Soon, all the little ones eagerly headed down the stairs, practically tripping over one another. Giggles and kisses invaded the hushed morning until Daddy quieted the crowd to pray. Tiffany cuddled Abigail, and I held Virginia Grace on my lap as we all bowed our heads.

This was our morning—the morning we gave Daddy our "hearts." He already had our hearts, of course, but this was the moment we showed him we really meant it. Today we gave him a keepsake—a representation of our hearts—a symbol of our trust in him. I'll remember this morning for the rest of my life. From the way Daddy smiled, I think he will, too.

———◆———

Over the last fifty years there have been great changes in our world. Technology has rapidly advanced as we've sent men to the moon and back, lived through the advent of the Internet, and celebrated the convenience of cell phones. In addition to our accomplishments, we have also seen other changes—changes that are not so heartening.

The decline of the strong, father-led family and the arrival of the modern *dating* model have culminated in an alarming increase in various forms of promiscuous and immoral premarital behavior. Slowly, as young men began to call on young women without the permission or involvement of their fathers, the picture of what we call dating took shape. When maidens were left unprotected by unwary or lazy fathers, a steady decline in chivalry and decorum assaulted the integrity of the courtship experience and turned it into a free-for-all. The most disturbing result was the ultimate attack on marriage: a skyrocketing divorce rate.

As God has awakened godly fathers and exposed the foolishness of modern dating to Christian families, we have been forced to analyze biblically how things should change. Many families have turned to a more Scriptural approach, one that includes family involvement and particularly includes the father.

Before our children reached the "dating" age, we made a decision to explore a more protected form of courtship. There are many different opinions of what courtship should look like, and each family will have to determine how this will play out in their own lives.

Last year, my daughters decided to give their father a special gift, one that symbolized their willingness to trust him with their hearts until the day he walked them down the aisle to entrust them to another in marriage. After the girls and I discussed their plan, I purchased a sterling silver engravable Bar Pin Charm Holder from www.jamesavery.com and had Malachi 4:6 engraved on it in soft script. Each of my daughters then purchased a unique heart-shaped charm and wrapped them separately. (I bought the younger girls' charms.)

As the monumental moment approached, the anticipation mounted as my four oldest daughters pondered the significance of the gift they were to give their kingly defender. In their spare moments, on decorative paper they thoughtfully penned expressions of their maidenly devotion to their father—words that expressed their willingness to obey God in remaining pure, verses of thanks for their father's protection, and declarations of their trust in his guidance into marriage.

———◆———

Tears welled in his fatherly eyes as he tenderly opened the packages containing our "hearts." A blanket of silence settled on the room. No one dared breathe. In the quietness, I could hear the crinkling of the delicate pink tissue as he untied the thin silken ribbon from the first package—the one containing my heart. One by one, we read him our prepared poems and letters—and, of course, Mama wept.

Share Your Heart

- ✜ Read Numbers 30:3-5 and discuss a father's responsibility and authority over his daughter. How does this Scripture pertain to a maiden's courtship and marriage?

- ✜ Look up the following Scriptures discussing **sinful jealousy**:
  - Genesis 4:3-7
  - Genesis 37:3-4
  - 1 Samuel 18:8
  - Job 5:2
  - Psalm 73:3
  - Proverbs 23:17

- ✜ Look up the following Scriptures discussing **godly jealousy**:

- 2 Corinthians 11:2
- Exodus 20:5
- Deuteronomy 32:16
- Isaiah 30:1-2
- Exodus 34:14
- Song of Solomon 8:6

❧ Discuss the difference between "sinful jealousy" (coveting that which God has forbidden us) and "godly jealousy" (coveting that which God has given or entrusted to us)?

❧ Have you ever become angry or annoyed because you thought your parents were being overprotective? How could your irritation make their job of defending and cherishing you more difficult? Do you believe your father has the right to be jealous over you? How will you feel about your husband's jealousy?

❧ Read Genesis 34:21-31. How might Dinah and her people have been spared such tragedy if she had stayed under the protection of her father and brothers?

❧ Read Psalm 51:10 and contemplate its meaning. Who creates a "clean" heart? Is it possible to do this on our own? What does it mean to have a "right spirit?"

❧ Read 1 Corinthians 7:34. It is possible that God will not call you to marriage. This is unlikely, however, since marriage and bearing children are normative in Scripture. If God does call you to remain single, what are some ways that you may serve God and your family and still remain within a biblical, womanly role? (1 Timothy 2:11-12, 1 Corinthians 14:34-35, Luke 2:36-38, 1 Corinthians 7:25)

Practical Tips for Guarding your Maidenly Heart:

1. Read God's Word and pray every day. Specifically ask God to help

you guard your heart. Pray for your father to make wise decisions regarding your future.

2. Avoid romance novels or discussions with other maidens regarding boys. When discussing your future role as a wife and mother, focus on preparing yourself biblically for your vocation. Keep away from discussions about romance, wedding fantasies, or eligible young men (whether they are godly or not).

3. Avoid being alone with a young man. It is best to fellowship while under the protection of your parents, within the environment of home and family.

4. Avoid fantasizing about who might be "Mr. Right." Stay on guard, especially when you sense that you may be attracted to a young man (or that he might be attracted to you). Remember your goal is to stay pure for the one you marry, both physically and emotionally.

5. Talk to your parents about your feelings. Let them know when you need prayer in a specific area. God has placed them over you for your protection—trust them and Him.

The following letters and poems were written by our McDonald maidens. It is our hope to read these expressions of faithfulness and trust upon the wedding day of each of our daughters. When that blessed day arrives, her father will remove the silver heart that has been kept so safe and deliver it, untainted, into the protective hand of her honorable groom.

Christa McDonald — age 19

My heart is like a flower. Its beginning was that of a tiny seed. It was safely planted in the soil of my family. God planted it there, and you, my father, have been appointed by God to water, guard, nurture, and train it.

I am giving you a symbol of my heart today. I want you to know I love and trust you to keep it safe. I know you will faithfully protect my purity and save my heart for the man God chose for me before the beginning of time. I will patiently wait for the day that he comes.

I am thankful for your commitment to keep my heart safe in the garden of our family. I am grateful for a father who loves me enough to keep out any intruders who might try to trample what God has planted. My heart is yours until the day you pluck a flower from the McDonald garden and give it away as a gift.

Thank you for taking your role as my father seriously. Thank you for protecting me and training me in the way I should go. I love you.

Tiffany McDonald — age 17

Upon this warm and special morn,

I have a delicate treasure,

For you, my father, with all my love,

I give with the greatest pleasure.

For this little silver trinket,

Shall always represent

The love between father and daughter

And the time together spent.

Into your hands I lay my heart

For you to watch and guard.

Keep it with you always,

And from the stranger barred.

I know you'll always keep it safe,

So I give you my heart today,

Until the day when with full blessing,

You give my heart away.

Melissa McDonald — *age 16*

This is my heart; I give it to you,

Until the day I wed.

Keep it safe and always true,

Until my vows are said.

Just as the silver is pure and bright,

I want my heart to be

Filled with the Savior's glorious light.

Hold it safe for me.

Love is a most precious gift,

Never let mine stray.

Keep it from a worldly drift

Until that special day.

Mold my heart, and train me well,

So one day I may be

Equipped to follow in your steps

And walk on steadily.

Jessica McDonald — age 13

Here is my whole heart,

Not just a small part.

I'm giving it all to you

To keep as a treasure,

Though not forever.

I'll leave that up to you.

There is only one.

Keep my heart for your son (in-law),

The one who my husband will be.

Gentle and true,

Just like you,

Saving his heart for me.

Written by Mama

for the three youngest McDonald maidens:

Abigail — 5

Virginia Grace — 2

Emma Katherine — 1

Though we're small, and can't yet rhyme,

Very soon there'll come a time

When like our sisters we'll vow to you,

A heart that's trusting, pure, and true.

And for now, there's much to do,

So train us well, knowing we love you!

Chapter 19

EXCUSE ME MA'AM, BUT YOUR DOCTRINE IS SHOWING

Not purloining, but shewing all good fidelity; that they may adorn the doctrine of God our Saviour in all things. (Titus 2:10)

M y high school choir teacher had a rule: we were never to wear our school uniforms outside of choir events, unless we were prepared to act like perfect ladies and gentlemen. If we were caught in public behaving in an unbecoming way while wearing our uniform, it exposed our school to ridicule and tainted our "good name." It also meant an automatic expulsion from choir. We took this charge seriously because we knew that along with the "honor" of being part of the choir we had a responsibility.

We fiercely guarded the reputation of our school name. As young maidens (and mothers), how much more duty we have to glorify the name of Christ as well as to honor that of our fathers and husbands—the *family* name the Lord has given us!

The state of our culture is a reflection of the condition of the Church. If Christians were living as God requires—if we were seeking to live our lives to glorify Him in every way—the godly result would be apparent in our particular society or culture.

Unfortunately, the graffiti of the world is often boldly smeared across the wedding gown of the Bride of Christ. What God describes as an abomination, the world labels "life partnership"; what God says is murder, society tragically names "choice"; and what God calls sin, the modern Church nicknames "Christian liberty."

As a result of such perverse notions of morality, we have also embraced a distorted view of womanhood. Feminine loveliness, apart from sensual lewdness, has been scoffed at. The undergarments of today's woman are revealed to the world, and she thinks she looks "cool." Every week she attends church dressed in clothing that should shame dear old Dad and cause Grandma to blush . . . yet no one flinches.

Unfortunately it's not just her slip that is showing; it's her doctrine. The way we view Christ and the Church is evident to the world by the way we respond to sin. How do we conduct our lives on a daily basis? Do we love our neighbor? Are you as a young maiden obeying your parents, being chaste and faithful to your future spouse? Are you as a wife and mother submitting to and loving your husband, diligently training your children and building up your house, rather than tearing it down?

Whether or not we really believe what we preach is revealed in the way husbands love their wives; the way families serve others and each other, reflecting the love of Christ in their daily lives; and the passionate manner in which we reject anything that opposes or exalts itself over the knowledge and truth of God's Word.

Now that you know what it means to be a true maiden of virtue, you will not be mired down in the distraction and filth of the world. The deception of modern androgynous womanhood will have lost its bizarre appeal, and you will find that you are better equipped to rise fearlessly above the evils of this age, to shine like a brilliant diamond—reflecting the rays of God's irresistible holiness to a lost and dying world. More than the making of lasting memories or the building of strong family relationships, I pray that you have caught a vision—a vision of sacred duty, a vision of feminine loveliness and purity, and a vision that communicates sound doctrine and joy in holiness.

May you, fair and virtuous maiden, be as a polished cornerstone in your

father's house. May you be zealous of good works, content in your calling, and joyful in the task that lies before you. May you gleam with the purity of the most perfect and priceless ruby, and may your faithfulness shine as you serve and glorify the Lord our God all the days of your life.

But speak thou the things which become sound doctrine:That the aged men be sober, grave, temperate, sound in faith, in charity, in patience. The aged women likewise, that they be in behaviour as becometh holiness, not false accusers, not given to much wine, teachers of good things; That they may teach the young women to be sober, to love their husbands, to love their children, To be discreet, chaste, keepers at home, good, obedient to their own husbands, that the word of God be not blasphemed. Young men likewise exhort to be sober minded. In all things shewing thyself a pattern of good works: in doctrine shewing uncorruptness, gravity, sincerity, Sound speech, that cannot be condemned; that he that is of the contrary part may be ashamed, having no evil thing to say of you. Exhort servants to be obedient unto their own masters, and to please them well in all things; not answering again; Not purloining, but shewing all good fidelity; that they may adorn the doctrine of God our Saviour in all things.

For the grace of God that bringeth salvation hath appeared to all men, Teaching us that, denying ungodliness and worldly lusts, we should live soberly, righteously, and godly, in this present world; Looking for that blessed hope, and the glorious appearing of the great God and our Saviour Jesus Christ;Who gave himself for us, that he might redeem us from all iniquity, and purify unto himself a peculiar people, zealous of good works. (Titus 2:1-14)

THE PAGES OF TIME:
A Multi-Generational Project

That the generation to come might know them, even the children which should be born; who should arise and declare them to their children: That they might set their hope in God, and not forget the works of God, but keep his commandments: And might not be as their fathers, a stubborn and rebellious generation; a generation that set not their heart aright, and whose spirit was not stedfast with God (Psalm 78:6-8).

E lizabeth turned the crisp pages tenderly as the sweet, musty scent of age and dried lavender flowers mingled in the air.

"Is this the story of when *you* were a maiden, Grandma?" Elizabeth asked curiously.

The silver-haired matriarch smiled, and her eyes welled with tears as sweet memories of tea time and Scripture reading came rushing back to her mind. She touched the dried flowers gently and inhaled the antique fragrance.

"No, Elizabeth," she replied affectionately. "This is the scrapbook your mother and I made together during our Maidens of Virtue study. She was fourteen and so full of questions. I felt terribly ill-equipped to teach her since no one had ever taught me. As God faithfully revealed His truths to us both, I learned what it meant to be a true maiden of virtue by watching God create one—your mother."

Elizabeth hugged her grandmother tightly. "Grandma!" she cried, "I want to become a maiden of virtue just like Mommy was. Do you think that's why Daddy wanted to marry her so much?"

"Yes, Elizabeth, I think your mother's purity and virtue probably had quite a bit to do with your father's interest in her." She smiled.

Elizabeth looked up teasingly. "Hey, Grandma," she said simply, "that makes you a *grand*-maiden!"

Create a Virtuous Maiden Scrapbook

As a butterfly net catches delicate winged treasures of spectacular beauty and glory, so will your scrapbook capture precious memories, thoughts, quotes, Bible passages, cards, photos, drawings, poems, and gems of knowledge that might otherwise have been lost. Have a disposable camera handy that is devoted to your tea or celebration times together. When the project is complete, you'll have a tangible keepsake of what you've learned and experienced. Those who learn best while doing hands-on projects will especially enjoy crafting this memory-making journal-scrapbook.

Please don't feel limited to the following list of suggested supplies. You can make your scrapbook as simple or extravagant as you wish. Please understand, however, that quality scrapbooks and acid-free paper and stickers will stand the test of time best. While construction paper may be inexpensive and colorful today, twenty years from now you may find it has faded or torn and yellowed or ruined your photos and keepsakes.

The Scrapbook

Acid free paper is paper that has at least a neutral or slightly alkaline pH. If you are using paper or materials that are not acid-free, over time the acid can harm your photos. Think of the way an old newspaper photograph looks. It becomes brittle, yellow, and faded.

- **A store-bought scrapbook**, made expressly for this type of project, will make your job simple. Look for one with acid-free pages and sturdy construction. (You can choose the quality according to your budget.)

- **A large binder** with a plastic cover that allows you to slide in your own decorated title page. Simply insert three-hole-punched, heavy stock paper directly into the binder, or use plastic sheet protectors to hold your pages.

ॐ **A pre-made journal** with heavy paper. Some of these are made with beautiful covers and decorative paper. They are generally inexpensive and would be a good choice for those who are on a budget yet want a scrapbook nice enough to set out for others to enjoy.

ॐ **A hand-bound scrapbook** is special. Some of you will be knowledgeable or adventurous enough to bind your own scrapbook. Make sure your pages are large enough to include photos and text on the same page. You may want at least ten pages (using front and back) for this study. Better yet, have a few extra pages to allow future generations to comment or make additions in the back.

Filling Your Scrapbook

For themes and project ideas for your scrapbook, refer to the "Memory Making Projects" section on page 201. Here is a list of supplies to embellish and beautify your project. I am also including a list of objects you will want to save and set aside before you begin. Remember that not all of these suggestions will be acid-free:

ॐ Decorative craft paper

ॐ Leftover scraps of wrapping paper

ॐ Stickers

ॐ Scraps of pretty fabric, ribbons, or lace

ॐ Photos

ॐ Poems or quotes pertaining to godly womanhood

ॐ Letters written to or received from godly women in your life

ॐ Magazine clippings

ॐ Drawings or paintings

ॐ Antique engravings or illustrations from books

ॐ Beautiful, feminine images cut out of old stationary, calendars, or greeting cards (examples: flowers, babies, leaves, herbs, dresses, ladies, carriages, perfume bottles, bonnets, Victorian style letters and graphics, tea cups, tea pots, baking scenes, and cottages)

- Old stamps
- Paper dolls
- Dried flowers (be sure to create a wax paper envelope, insert the flower, and seal it to protect the page from degrading)
- Multi-colored acid-free scrapbooking pens (Calligraphy pens are nice.)
- Stamps depicting feminine images of nature and beauty

You can also simply print whatever you want from your computer, in whatever font you like. For a more elegant look, you may want to use an off-white or decorative paper and tear the edges after printing.

Tuck these treasures away in a few large manila envelopes and save them until they're needed. This way, you won't waste precious time in the middle of your study looking for just the right embellishments—they'll be at your fingertips.

If you are doing this study with a group, you may find it a better use of your time to work on the craft portion of the scrapbook at home and concentrate on the actual study during your time as a group.

Remember, you are making memories. Don't treat this book like a workbook. Take your time, read aloud together, and drink in the truth and poetry of Scripture. Reason together, pray together, laugh together, and be prepared to be transformed together!

Imagine what a blessing it would be to have a scrapbook detailing the thoughts and prayers of your Christian great-great-grandmother as she learned at the knee of her own mother. Envision reading journal entries or poems and browsing through drawings, photos, or keepsakes that were special to your ancestors.

Making a scrapbook is optional for this study; however, a visual keepsake of this sort can be a treasure that is passed on to future generations along with the heritage of godly maidenhood that it represents.

MEMORY-MAKING PROJECTS
(Includes Scrapbook Page Themes)

1. Virtuous Women from the Past

Choose a historical figure whose godly, feminine traits you would like to emulate. Why do you think she is a good role model, and how may she have influenced others for Christ? You may use the suggestions below, or choose your own. Discuss with your mother the reasons for your choice.

- Read a biography, or glean information from the encyclopedia or Internet about her life. Make sure you use good sources and take plenty of notes. Write down specific anecdotes or sketches from her life. Was she married? How many children did she have? Was she persecuted or martyred for her faith? What makes you think she was a godly woman?

- Host a "Historical Women Tea Party" using the guidelines and ideas from the Literary Luncheon on page 211. Be sure to take lots of pictures and include them in your scrapbook page for this section. You could even host a follow-up party, inviting your guests to make a scrapbook page similar to what you've done.

❧ Draw or paint a picture of your historical figure, print an image of her from the Internet, or trace her likeness from an old book.

❧ Write a poem about your heroine and her virtues.

❧ Using either your best handwriting, calligraphy, or a pretty font printed from your computer; add quotes from this woman to your scrapbook pages.

❧ Look up Scripture verses that demonstrate the godly, spiritual traits of your chosen heroine. Embellish your scrapbook page with these verses.

❧ Decorate the rest of the page with time-period-appropriate stickers, lace, or other trimmings. Be creative!

Suggested Heroines:

❧ Lady Jane Grey

❧ Amy Carmichael

❧ Anne Boleyn

❧ Katie Luther

❧ Elisabeth Elliot

❧ Monica (St. Augustine's mother)

❧ Susannah Wesley

❧ Dolly Madison

❧ Anne of Bohemia (Wife of Richard II)

❧ Anne Bradstreet (Good Queen Maud)

❧ Clara Barton

❧ Gladys Alyward

❧ Florence Nightingale

2. *Family Traditions*

In Chapter 3 Agnes loved her home in Eisleben. Paint or draw a picture of the home that *you* love. Include things you love about that home (a special tree or flower bush, a quilt, a special cozy room, your spot at the dinner table). Draw a picture or glue a photo of your family somewhere on the page. Write a few paragraphs about why this home is special to you. You may include special memories or events (the birth of a sibling, a time you were ill, a particular celebration). Remember that someone else may not be able to understand what makes it so special to you, so be descriptive.

3. Make a Recipe File or Family Heirloom Cookbook

There are several recipes I make for my family that have been passed down through several generations. Some have a story to be told; others had a story, but it was lost in a previous generation, though the recipe was tasty enough to be remembered and used years later.

For each of my daughters (and daughters-in-law) I plan to create a family recipe book or box before they marry. This will include all of our favorite meals, desserts, dressings, and sauces. It will include the stories that are remembered and those that have yet to be created.

You can do this for your own family. Think of all the recipes that have become traditions or favorites in your own family. Interview your mother, grandmother, or aunts, asking for special family recipes and their history.

Be sure to take the best recipe with the very best story and create a fun scrapbook page. Decorate your page with graphics or stickers of aprons, spoons, measuring cups, pots, pans, stoves, or pies. Have a "kitchen theme" that will fit well with your recipe. If the recipe is from a grandmother or other family member, ask them to hand write a comment about the recipe and sign it. Then cut out their quote with decorative scissors and place it on your scrapbook page. Remind them that humorous stories can be fun, too!

4. Brothers and Sisters

Write down the names of each of your siblings on a separate piece of paper. If you are an only child, you can list the names of cousins, young relatives, or other surrogates the Lord has provided. On each page write some of your favorite memories with or of that sibling. Your stories can be humorous, touching, or serious, but make sure they are God-honoring.

Make a scrapbook page that includes a picture of each of your siblings. Write a short paragraph describing their good character qualities and things you'll miss once you are all grown. Be sure to record at least one experience where God showed you how important your siblings are in your life.

5. *Powdered and Perfumed*

Create a "Powdered and Perfumed" page. Find Scripture verses pertaining to cleanliness and purity, and place them in hand-drawn "bath bubbles." Write out short statements that were meaningful to you during this section of study. Be sure to communicate why you believe cleanliness is important.

Use graphics, photos, stickers, or drawings of things pertaining to the bath. Decorate further with dried lavender, rose petals, or decorative soap wrappers.

Graphic or drawing suggestions:

Old-fashioned bathtub, shampoo bottles, perfume bottles, herbs, soap, towels, bubbles, bathrobe, Victorian dressing gown, vanity table, slippers, rubber duck, scrub brush, water faucet, clothes line, wash bucket

6. *A Daughter's Heart*

Compose a poem or letter for your father describing your trust in his guidance. Let him know by your words that you are committed to remaining pure and are thankful for his protection and leadership.

You could take the idea from chapter 18 and plan to give a symbolic "heart" to your father as a gift. www.jamesavery.com has various unique and reasonably priced heart charms to choose from. Ask your mother if she is interested in contributing to your project by buying a chain or pin from which the charm can dangle. It will be a great blessing for him to have a reminder that you have willingly surrendered your "heart" to him.

Make a "Kingly Protector" scrapbook page. Fill it with father-daughter mementos. Include poems, letters, photos, postcards, or other reminders of your relationship. Be sure to include special photos of the giving or receiving of heart charms, promise rings, or other symbolic gifts.

7. Courtship and Marriage

Write a short letter to God indicating your trust in Him and your faithfulness to your future spouse (whether a husband or the Lord, if God calls you to remain unmarried). Decorate it with beautiful fonts, stickers, flowers or other embellishments and place it in your scrapbook. Include Scriptures that relate to purity, trust, faithfulness, contentment, and joy. Pray that God would guard your future husband's heart and help him to remain pure in thought and deed for you as well. Ask the Lord to bless your womb and give you children to train up for His glory.

WARNING! Be careful to guard your heart against obsessing. Remember that God is sovereign and it *is* possible that He may call you to single maidenhood. Remember, God will not only equip and give you special grace for whatever He calls you to do, He will also give you joy in it! Therefore, be content. Ask your mother if she feels it is wise for you to do this project. If it might cause you to fall into temptation, it is better that you skip this one.

8. A Maiden's Book of Prayer
(by Lady Jessica McDonald)

Do you ever find it difficult to keep your mind from wandering when you pray? Are you racked with guilt because you can't seem to keep your thoughts from drifting? Do you find that you just can't seem to stay focused?

I remember kneeling beside my bed with determination, clasping my hands together, and trying fervently to pray to our Heavenly Father. No sooner had I begun than I found myself thinking about the guests we were expecting the next day and the book my mother had promised to pick up at the library.

I was heartsick when I realized I had been in a "conversation" with Jesus Christ, the King of Kings, and I had *ignored* Him to think about frivolous activities. Then one day as I knelt to pray, I suddenly had a thought. Why not write down my prayers in a little book? Then I could read them aloud without my mind wandering. I would also have a record of my times with Jesus to refer to later. I would be able to see where God was working in my life and where He was answering my prayers!

I found that writing down my prayers gave me the ability to reflect on what I wanted to say, rather than simply blurting out the first thing that popped into my head. It also helped me to address Jesus with reverence and awe. Even though He is our truest and most loyal friend, Jesus is not our *buddy*. When it occurred to me that Jesus is my Sovereign King and Lord and that I wouldn't speak to an earthly king like he was my buddy, I had to wonder why would I could treat Jesus like He was? The Lord is the "friend that sticks closer than a brother," but He is also a holy and awesome God, and deserves our reverence! (Proverbs 18:24)

Suggestions for getting started:

- Purchase a store-bought journal, a diary, or a clean spiral notebook. Or, if you really want to get creative, bind and decorate your own little book. When Elizabeth Tudor was a little girl she embroidered a cover for her father's prayer book. It might be enjoyable to attempt a similar project.

- If your prayer book doesn't already include a bookmark, paste a thin silk ribbon inside the back binding so you can easily find your page for the next entry.

- Find a quiet spot to write out your prayers each day. After you have written out everything you want to say to the Lord, pray your words aloud to Him. I prefer writing my prayers like letters, as it makes me feel more like Jesus is right there in the room listening to me (which He is). Here is an example:

Dear Lord Jesus,

You are so wonderful and good. Forgive me for the times I was short with my sister today. Please help me to be obedient to my parents and to have a good attitude when I am corrected. Help me to be cheerful when asked to do chores—and even remind me to do things without being asked. Thank you for healing Couzin Lucy so quickly. Please show Uncle Alfred his sins and his need for You as a Savior—draw him to Yourself, Lord. I love you and thank you for all you are and all you are doing in my life. Amen.

Come up with your own personal prayers to the Lord, but there are also a lot of good examples of prayer in the Bible. Study the book of Psalms, where David cries out to God. Reflect upon the Lord's Prayer. This is a wonderful start and will bless you as you realize the importance and loveliness of a consistent prayer life.

9. A Mother-Maiden Journal
(by Lady Tiffany McDonald)

Every young maiden desires someone after whose image she can sculpt her life. Too often, though, she may look in the direction of the teen magazine, movie stars, or fashion world for a model. Steadily she is indoctrinated by airbrushed images of artificial "beauty" and a gnawing desire for physical "perfection." When a young maiden strives to meet the standards of the world, she will often be left disillusioned, depressed, and confused.

She needs an anchor, a godly role model to whom she can turn for wisdom, advice, and prayer. She should look no further than her own home. The mother of a maiden knows her own daughter better than anyone else. She was charged by God to train her up and to be her guide, to teach her what God says makes a woman lovely, and to help her properly define a "healthy self-image." As a young woman blossoms into maidenhood, her mother should be the one teaching her about virtue, purity, and feminine loveliness.

Sometimes a young girl has a hard time *saying* what is on her mind. It may be easier to pour out her prayers, questions, and even her woes to her mother on paper, rather than to voice them aloud. As her body changes, simmering hormones may ignite mood swings and even unprompted tears. She will need advice and counsel on how to battle her flesh in this specific area, and it may be less intimidating to write her concerns down, rather than to describe them face to face.

How to Begin

Purchase a lovely journal for you and your daughter to co-author. It does not have to be expensive, but make sure it is well-made so that it will last. If you have time, craft one yourself, including your daughter in the project.

Begin your journal with Scripture. Find a verse that represents godly womanhood. Each night, have your daughter write a page, sharing events from her day, struggles in her life, dreams she may have, or truths the Lord has shown her. Remind her to include any prayer requests and questions she may have.

After her daily entry, have her return the journal to you so that you can read it, ponder what you've read, and respond. Pray for her prayer requests and ask the Lord to show you what wisdom He will give you to share with her. On the next page write a reply full of love, advice, admonishment, encouragement, Scripture, and prayers. Write "love notes" to one another. Be sure to include plenty of encouragement in the areas you see her growing. Make a diligent attempt to do this every day. If you cannot fit it into your schedule, do it at least three times a week.

Be sure to keep the journal. As your daughter grows, both of you will be able to look back through the precious pages of the journal you shared and see how your gentle maiden has grown, what God has brought her through, and how He has answered her prayers. The love and guidance that she may not have fully appreciated or understand at the time will become clearer to her as she matures and looks back on your words. You will be blessed by having a physical reminder of your part in the training of her maiden-years. She will be thankful and content, and she will rise and call you blessed (Proverbs 31:28).

A LITERARY MAIDEN LUNCHEON
for Mothers and Daughters

These are not books, lumps of lifeless paper, but minds alive on the shelves. From each of them goes out its own voice and just as the touch on our set will fill the room with music, so by taking down one of these volumes and opening it, one can call into range the voice of a man far distant in time and space, and hear him speaking to us, mind to mind, heart to heart. – Gilbert Highet, Scottish-American classicist (1906-78)

W e have discussed books several times during the course of this study. There's a reason for that. A great work of literature stretches the mind of a maiden, challenging her to think and expand her horizons. An intelligent maiden is discerning with the books she chooses and analyzes everything she reads through the lens of Scripture.

A profitable way to examine and explore various works of literature is to join or host a literary club. Here we have suggested hosting a Literary Maiden Luncheon which will combine your study of maidenhood with a delightful luncheon focused on the classic literature piece of your choice.

A Theme

Create a theme for your luncheon using a feminine character from a classic work of literature. Ask each of your guests to read the selected book beforehand. This way you can have a worthwhile discussion during your luncheon. Some suggestions are:

Little Women or *Old-Fashioned Girl* by Louisa May Alcott

Jane Eyre by Charlotte Brontë

Pride and Prejudice by Jane Austen

From Dark to Dawn by Elizabeth Charles

Stepping Heavenward by Elizabeth Prentiss

Mother by Kathleen Norris

Anne of Green Gables by L. M. Montgomery

Invitations

What better way to encourage mother-daughter activities than by practicing hospitality together? Whether you choose store-bought or handmade invitations, make sure they are feminine and written to include both mother and daughter. You could address it with a maidenly flair by writing something like this:

> *Lady Katherine and her gentle daughter, Lady Anne, request the honor of your company for a Literary Maiden Luncheon at the Smith Castle...*

When addressing your envelopes, write the names of your guests in ways that speak of their godliness and femininity:

> *Lady Kimberly and her virtuous maiden daughter, Lady Hannah*

Place Cards

Make a place card for each guest that resembles a miniature book.

Create a mock cover on the computer by copying an antique book cover on a copy machine, creating one on a desktop publishing program (like Microsoft® Publisher), or by painting or decorating one yourself. Use a copy machine to shrink it to the desired size for your mini book, copying it onto card stock or some other heavy paper.

Once your cover is complete, fold it in half to resemble a book. Cut several pages for your book from plain white paper, according to the size of your cover, and staple it together in the binding area to resemble a book (do not attach it to the book cover yet). Glue a thin piece of silky ribbon along the inside binding of your book cover (leaving about an inch hanging out the top) to make a permanent book mark. Place your bound paper inside the book cover and glue the first and last pages to the inside cover.

On the first page of your "place-book," write:

This book is dedicated to _____. (Place the name of your guest in the blank.)

This becomes your guest's place card and a special token for her to take home. You may also include a favorite verse of Scripture or write a special note of thanks, encouragement, or poem within its pages for a useful keepsake that can later be used as a book mark.

If you are pressed for time, a nice homemade or store-bought bookmark would do just as nicely.

> Reading a great work of literature can truly be likened to having a conversation with a great mind.
>
> JENNIE CHANCEY

A Gracious Hostess

It may be a good idea to purchase a good etiquette book. There are several suggestions in the Reading Suggestions in the back of this book.

When the day comes, greet each of your guests personally at the door and welcome them by saying, "Thank you for coming! I'm so pleased you are here!" Introduce those who have never met. Offer to take their coats and show them where they can put their purses or other belongings.

Offer them something to drink and show them where they may sit.

Begin your luncheon with a prayer. If you plan to ask someone else to pray, be sure to ask her ahead of time. Be sure to mingle with all of your guests. Don't spend all of your time with a few "favorite friends." As your friends leave, see them to the door and be sure to thank them for coming.

Menu and Atmosphere

Plan your menu carefully. You may want to research what your book character would have served during her time period. Study what she would have served for lunch, to drink, and for dessert. What kind of music might she have enjoyed with her guests? What games might she have played?

Decorating

Be sure to make it a special occasion. Fresh flowers, cloth napkins, candles, a formal table cloth, and other "special occasion" accessories may be in order. Napkin rings can be made very simply, yet give an air of elegance and creativity by using a fresh flower tied with a strip of lace, or simply tie a thin piece of ribbon into a bow around your napkins. For an elegant literary centerpiece, use a stack of antique books sprinkled with flower petals sitting upon a lace doily.

One fun way to decorate for a Literary Luncheon is to find wonderful short quotes from your book and copy them into a word processing program. Choose quotes that have to do with godly maidenhood or womanhood. Once you have them typed in, choose a decorative, yet legible font. Alternatively, you can practice your best cursive handwriting or calligraphy for this project. Copy the quotes onto off-white resume paper, parchment-style paper, or something similar. Gently tear the edges of each quote to give them an aged look. You can burn the edges or "gild" them with metallic gold craft paint. Scatter your quotes, along with some sweet smelling flower petals and 1-2 inch strips of lace ribbon upon the tables or serving area. A few scented candles make a nice addition as well.

Book Discussion

Create ahead of time a list of discussion questions pertaining to your literature choice. Discuss your chosen character's honorable qualities, but don't forget to consider her weaknesses as well.

To give you an idea of what types of questions might be profitable, here are some sample discussion questions for *Jane Eyre* by Charlotte Brontë, excerpted from the article *Hosting a Literary Tea* by Jennie Chancey:

SAMPLE QUESTION SHEET FOR *JANE EYRE*:

1. Read a short biography of Charlotte Brontë (you might even print a sheet from an online source to share). Do you feel the author brought her own experiences to bear upon her writing? Does Jane reflect Charlotte Brontë's own struggles and dreams?

2. How do we get to know the characters through Jane's eyes? Note how her perspective matures from childhood to adulthood.

3. How does Jane treat Mr. Rochester? Compare this with how other women in the story treat him.

4. How do Jane's spiritual beliefs affect her relationships with others (Mrs. Reed, her cousins, friends at school, the headmistress, Mr. Rochester, St. John Rivers, etc.)?

5. Do you think Jane makes the right choice when she runs away from Mr. Rochester after discovering his secret?

6. Do you think St. John's offer to Jane is a good one? Why or why not?

7. How does Jane reconcile with Mr. Rochester, and how does this demonstrate her unwillingness to compromise her faith and her moral convictions?

8. What do you think of the final paragraph in the book?

9. If you had to name one theme that ties all of *Jane Eyre* together, what would it be?

10. Which character is your favorite, and why?

The directions for hosting a Literary Maiden Luncheon can be modified and used to host a Historical Women Tea as well. See Project #1 on page 201.

READING AND RESOURCE LIST

A Woman of Significance by Donna Morley

Aunt Jane's Hero by Elizabeth Prentiss

All the Way Home by Mary Pride

Attitudes of a Transformed Heart by Martha Peace

Authentic Beauty by Leslie Ludy

Basket of Flowers by Christoph Von Schmid

Beautiful Girlhood by Mabel Hale

Beautiful in God's Eyes by Elizabeth George

Beauty and the Pig: A Study of Godly Beauty by Pam Forster

Biblical Womanhood in the Home by Nancy Leigh DeMoss

Christian Charm Course by Emily Hunter

Christian Courtship vs. the Dating Game by Jim West

Christian Modesty and the Public Undressing of America by Jeff Pollard

Courtship of Sarah McLean, The by the Castleberrys

Daughters of Destiny edited by Noelle Wheeler

Dressing with Dignity by Colleen Hammond

Emotional Purity by Heather Arnel Paulsen

Female Piety by John A. James

Feminine Appeal by Carolyn Mahaney

Five Women of the English Reformation by Paul F. M. Zahl

From Dark to Dawn by Elizabeth Rundle Charles

God's Priceless Woman by Wanda Sanseri

Golden Thoughts of Mother, Home and Heaven by Gene Fedele

Her Hand in Marriage by Doug Wilson

Hidden Art of Homemaking by Edith Schaeffer

Hind's Feet on High Places by Hannah Hurnard

His Chosen Bride by Jennifer Lamp

In My Father's House by Tamara and Naomi Valine

Let Me Be a Woman by Elizabeth Elliot

Letters on Practical Subjects to a Daughter by W. B. Sprague

Making Brothers and Sisters Best Friends by the Mally Family

Mary Bunyan: Blind Daughter of John Bunyan by Sallie Rochester Ford

More than a Hope Chest by Amber Moeller

Mother by Kathleen Norris

Of Knights and Fair Maidens by Jeff and Danielle Myers

Old-Fashioned Courtship and How it Works by Jeff and Marge Barth

Passion and Purity by Elisabeth Elliot

Pearl Maiden by H. Rider Haggard

Peep Behind the Scenes by O. F. Walton

Perfect Date, The by Joshua & Kerry Williams

Polished Cornerstones by Pam Forster

Practical Godliness: The Ornament of All Religion by Vincent Alsop

Quest for Love by Elisabeth Elliot

Quest for Meekness and Quietness of Spirit, A by Matthew Henry

Quest for the High Places by Natalie Nyquist

Scrapbooking for Beginners (video) www.memorylanevideosonline.com

Social Graces by Ann Platz

Stepping Heavenward by Elizabeth Prentiss

Talks to Girls by Eleanor Hunter

The Hope Chest: A Legacy of Love by Rebekah Wilson

Total Image: Personal Development Inside & Out by Lynda Murphy

Training Our Daughters to Be Keepers at Home by Ann Ward

Verses of Virtue compiled by Beall Phillips

Waiting for Her Isaac by The Castleberrys

Westminster Shorter Catechism with Study Notes by G. I. Williamson

Winsome Womanhood: Daybreak by Shelley Noonan

Wise Woman, The by George MacDonald

Young Lady's Guide to the Harmonious Development of Christian Character by Harvey Newcomb

Your Girl by Vicki Courtney (for Moms only!)

WHERE DO YOU FIND FEMININE CLOTHES THAT ARE MODEST?

I am frequently asked where a mother can find modest, beautiful clothing for her daughter without sewing it herself. I admit it is more difficult than it should be, but thankfully there are many businesses that realize not everyone wants to expose themselves in public.

I have compiled a list of websites that sell modest, feminine clothing and shoes. Some are cottage industries that offer simple hand-made jumpers, children's clothes, and aprons, while others sell lovely patterns or elegant feminine clothing fashioned after days gone by, while still others are larger companies or chains offering beautifully classic dresses and skirts and lovely embroidered blouses and sweaters.

Though I have briefly visited each of these sites to check for suitability, please take personal responsibility and exercise caution while viewing any website or link that each may contain. Also, be aware that some sites which carry beautiful, modest clothing also offer clothing that is not so modest. Use the principles that you learned in our study to choose your wardrobe prayerfully.

http://pureinheart.hypermart.net/

www.aprilcornell.com

www.bakerlane.com

www.bedfordfair.com/pagebuilder/

www.chadwicks.com

www.coldwatercreek.com

www.ullapopken.com

www.commonsensepatterns.com

www.considerthelilies.us

www.covenantweddingsource.com

www.daddys-little-princess.com

www.eddiebauer.com

www.frenchtoast.com

www.hannahanderson.com

www.hannahlise.com

www.jmarco.com

www.landsend.com

www.liliesapparel.com

www.littletouchofelegance.com

www.modestclothing.bizhosting.com

www.modestpatterns.com

www.plowsharesltd.com

www.sensibility.com

www.silhouettes.com

www.simplyskirts.com

www.theclassicprincess.com

www.wardrobeclassics.com

www.wendysmodestdress.com

www.wholesomewear.com (modest swimwear)

www.willowridgecatalog.com

www.worksoftheheart.com

STACY MCDONALD

*S*tacy is the wife of James McDonald, the homeschooling mother of nine blessings, and the editor-in-chief of *Homeschooling Today*® www.homeschoolingtoday.com and *Family Reformation*™ www.fami lyreformation.com magazines. She lives in Texas where she serves her family and assists her husband with their family publications and the management of their bookstore www.booksonthepath.com. As time allows, Stacy enjoys speaking to women on subjects pertaining to wives, mothers, and daughters. Her special passion is sharing God's truth regarding a wife's godly role in marriage, contented motherhood, and the true meaning of feminine biblical beauty.

If you are interested in having the McDonald family speak or give a seminar at your group or organization please call or write for more information.

Books on the Path
PO BX 436
Barker, TX 77413

281-492-6050
info@raisingmaidens.com